THE INTERIOR OF ST MAGNUS CATHEDRAL

from the painting by Stanley Cursiter, R.S.A.

THE NEW
ORKNEY
BOOK

Compiled and edited by

JOHN SHEARER
W. GROUNDWATER
J. D. MACKAY

NELSON

THOMAS NELSON AND SONS LTD
36 Park Street London W1
P.O. Box 336 Apapa Lagos
P.O. Box 25012 Nairobi
77 Coffee Street San Fernando Trinidad

THOMAS NELSON (AUSTRALIA) LTD
597 Little Collins Street Melbourne

THOMAS NELSON & SONS (SOUTH AFRICA) (PROPRIETARY) LTD
P.O. Box 9881 Johannesburg

THOMAS NELSON AND SONS (CANADA) LTD
81 Curlew Drive Don Mills Ontario

THOMAS NELSON AND SONS
Copewood and Davis Streets Camden 3, N.J.

———

© *John Shearer* 1966

First published 1966

Printed in Great Britain by
Thomas Nelson (Printers) Ltd, London and Edinburgh

PREFACE

THE ORKNEY BOOK, 'prepared for use in the schools of Orkney' by a group of young Orcadian scholars resident in Edinburgh, and published in 1909, is perhaps the best known volume in our native Orkney literature. We who first read it in school days remember well its lucidity and charm, and the interest which it fostered in our islands. But the book is long out of print and the present volume has been written in the hope that new readers will find pleasure in the story of Orkney.

Among our many contributors Stanley Cursiter, R.S.A., occupies a unique place. He was responsible for the decorative work in the 1909 volume, and now again he has given much advice and assistance, including the cover design and permission to reproduce in colour two Orkney paintings.

The first part of the book has been written almost entirely by Orcadians who have studied the history and natural history of the islands and who readily undertook to prepare the various sections. To Dr W. Douglas Simpson, librarian of Aberdeen University, we are greatly indebted for the chapter on the Cathedral of St Magnus.

Part Two has been planned to bring together modern writing in prose and verse about Orkney. It contains passages from the work of seven Orkney authors and poets, some of whom have won a national reputation, while all hold an honoured place in their native county.

J. S.

ACKNOWLEDGMENTS

The editors wish to acknowledge the gracious permission of Her Majesty the Queen to reproduce in colour the painting *Interior of St Magnus Cathedral*, by Stanley Cursiter.

Thanks are due to authors, publishers, and private individuals for the courtesy with which numerous requests have been received, and for permission to print copyright material as follows: Eric Linklater, Macmillan and Co Ltd. and A. D. Peters for passages respectively from *The Man on my Back* and *The Ultimate Viking*; Mrs Willa Muir, and Faber and Faber Ltd. for four poems from *Collected Poems*, and The Hogarth Press Ltd. for passages from *An Autobiography*, both by Edwin Muir; T. Spence for *Life and Work in Moorland Orcadia* by John Spence; R. Learmonth for *The Dwelling House* by John Firth; Dr D. Maclaren for *The Selkie that deud no' forget* by W. Traill Dennison; Robert Rendall for three poems; George Mackay Brown for two poems; Hudson's Bay Record Society for a quotation from *The History of the Hudson's Bay Company*; Erlend R. S. Clouston for a quotation from *The History of Orkney* by J. Storer Clouston; John Murray Ltd. for a quotation from *Edward Wilson of the Antarctic*.

Grateful acknowledgment is made to the Holyrood Amenity Trust for assistance in producing in colour the *Interior of St Magnus Cathedral* and to Mrs J. M. Archer for kind permission and help with the painting *Westray* by Stanley Cursiter; also to the following for pictures reproduced from photographs: W. Marr, Nos. 1, 4, 7, 8, 12, 13, 14, 15, 20, 22, 23, 24, 29; W. Hourston, 6, 10, 16, 26, 27, 28; R. Miller, 5, 9, 17, 19, 21, 25; W. R. Flett, 18; N. Firth, 2, 3; and *The Scotsman*, 11. Thanks are also due to John Bartholomew and Son Ltd. for the endpaper map, and to Miss M. Gordon and Miss J. Robertson for the population map on page 87.

Finally, we record our thanks to the two groups who have given maximum help: the writers whose names appear in the table of Contents, Part I, and Appendix, and Orkney Education Authority, whose assurance of support has made publication possible.

CONTENTS

PART ONE

PART TWO

ILLUSTRATIONS

PART ONE

THE FIRST SETTLERS

The Stone Age

THE first men to reach Orkney, perhaps four or five thousand years ago, looked on islands similar in size and shape to those of today, but otherwise very different. Before these explorers lay no pleasant green fields, no cattle browsing in flowery meadows, and no farmhouses of grey stone with stackyards and outbuildings. Instead they would have seen great stretches of moorland and innumerable pools of water and large lochs; a grim and inhospitable land.

These early settlers must have been bold and skilful seamen. There is some evidence to suggest that they came to the islands not only with their wives and families, but with cattle and perhaps sheep as well. Their boats must have been very primitive by our standards, and crossing the Pentland Firth would have been as dangerous then as it is today.

It is almost certain that these *megalithic* people, as they are called, originated somewhere in the Mediterranean. Their chief monuments are the famous burial cairns which are probably the most interesting feature of Orcadian prehistory, but cairns, not unlike types found in Orkney, can also be seen in Sicily, Malta, Spain and Brittany, as well as along the west coast of England and Scotland. This would lead us to suppose that the megalithic people came from the eastern Mediterranean, and there may, indeed, be some links between Maeshowe and the famous shaft graves of Mycenae in Greece.

The cairns were the burial places of chieftains and, before they were rifled by successive waves of invaders, they probably contained articles made of precious metals. The Norsemen forced their way into Maeshowe three thousand years after its erection and inscribed runic writings on its walls. These runes refer to a great treasure which was probably found in the Mound itself and then buried at some considerable distance from it, although experts differ as to what may have been the exact location of this treasure trove.

The cairns to be found in Orkney may be divided into round-chambered cairns of the Maeshowe type, long cairns, and stalled cairns.

The most famous cairn in Orkney is Maeshowe in Stenness, but Quoyness in Sanday, Blackhammar cairn in Rousay, and the Stalled Cairn on the Holm of Papa Westray are also worthy of note. Indeed, there is such an abundance of Neolithic burial places in Orkney that even a list of them would run into two or three pages.

Maeshowe

It may be claimed that Maeshowe is the finest megalithic tomb in the British Isles. In outward appearance it is a circular mound, 24 feet high and 115 feet in diameter, and it stands on a level space of ground varying in width from 40 feet to 70 feet. This, in turn, is surrounded by a shallow ditch which is 20 feet to 60 feet wide.

The entrance to the cairn is a narrow passage 36 feet long and about 3 feet wide. As it is only 4 feet 6 inches high in parts, an adult has to crouch to reach the inside. The main chamber is 15 feet square, but leading off from it on three sides there is in each a rectangular recess, and the openings to these recesses are 3 feet above the level of the floor. Doubtless, when the cairn was in use, the bones and ashes of the dead were placed in the recesses together with articles of value for use in the spirit world.

The masonry of the cairn is astonishing when we consider that its builders would have had no modern tools or materials like cement. The stones are fitted so perfectly together that one can only say that the whole structure must have been the work of a master builder.

In Hoy, another Neolithic grave of exceptional interest is to be found. This is the famous Dwarfie Stone which lies in a valley surrounded by rocky precipices. The Stone is a block of sandstone 28 feet long, about 14 feet wide, and 8 feet or more in depth; a passage and two cells have been hollowed out of it.

According to an ancient fable, this stone was the handiwork of a giant and his wife who were later imprisoned inside it by a second giant who wished to make himself master of Hoy. His evil designs were thwarted, however, as the first giant was able to gnaw his way out of the roof of the chamber in which he had been imprisoned, leaving a hole as a permanent record of his escape.

Skara Brae

While it is interesting to learn something about the burial customs of these early Orcadians, it is even more fascinating to find out just how they lived. Fortunately they have also left behind a more or less complete Stone Age settlement for us to study at Skara Brae in Sandwick.

The village is built on the margin of the beach at the Bay of Skaill, and, for thousands of years, it was buried beneath the sand. Then in 1850, during a severe storm accompanied by very high tides, part of the sand heap was washed away, exposing the walls of a stone building. Even at that time it was realised that the structure might be of considerable interest and some of the sand was dug away. But it was only in 1927 that proper excavation work began, under the guidance of Prof. V. Gordon Childe, one of the greatest archaeologists in Europe. Soon scholars all over the world were thrilled to hear that an entire prehistoric village had been found in Orkney, with houses in which even the furniture was intact.

The settlement of Skara Brae consists of a group of ten stone huts, the walls of which are, in many places, 9 feet high. The huts are connected by a maze of stone-built passages and covered alleyways so that, when viewed on a plan, they appear to be squeezed together in a haphazard manner. Each individual house is roughly rectangular in shape, with rounded corners, and is about 15 feet square. The entrance to each hut is a low and narrow hole, fitted with stone jambs and bar-holes for holding a door in place.

Inside the huts various articles of furniture have survived, being made of stone and not wood. Among these furnishings we can pick out stone dressers with two shelves, wall cupboards, box beds made entirely of stone, boxes for holding shell fish, and seats near the central hearths. The reason why stone and not wood was used for the making of furniture was because Orkney was as treeless in Neolithic times as it is today.

It is unlikely that a modern man would be impressed by Skara Brae if he could travel backwards in time and pay a visit to the village while it was still inhabited. He might well be overpowered by the smell inside the huts, for the floors would be strewn with bones of dead animals, limpet shells, and rotting scraps of fish. Then, too, he would find refuse heaped high on the roofs until the whole village would resemble a large mound with smoke from hidden fires emerging here and there through holes. He would be able to visit the various huts without going out-of-doors as the passageways, or village streets, would be covered over.

By examining the refuse from the huts, archaeologists have been able to tell what kind of food the Skara Brae villagers ate. Immense numbers of limpet shells and bones of cattle and sheep were found in the kitchen midden, but there were no traces of grain. It is probable that the staple diet consisted of beef and mutton, but when there was a scarcity of domestic animals the villagers lived mainly on shellfish.

Many animals would have been killed off in the early autumn as it would have been almost impossible to keep them alive during the long, damp winter without crops of hay or straw.

The tools used by the Skara Brae people were made of stone or bone, and of these flint scrapers were particularly numerous. The stone axe-heads had ground edges and some of them were mounted with the aid of antler socket-pieces. Most of the piercing tools were formed from the bones of deer, sheep, and oxen, while the flatter bones of oxen were used as shovels. The presence of deer's antlers and bones, and the fact that some of the pins found on the site were made of walrus ivory, prove that deer and walrus were common in Orkney in pre-historic times.

The pottery found at Skara Brae is very coarse and badly fired, indicating that the villagers were not very good craftsmen. Most of the pots have been built up with rings of clay laid one on the top of the other, known as coil pottery today. Parallel lines, strips, and blobs of clay and chevrons are used as patterns on the sides of the pots, but these designs are often very primitive.

The Standing Stones

Finally, in dealing with the early inhabitants of Orkney, we must not forget the great circles of Standing Stones and isolated monoliths which may be found in fields here and there throughout the islands. The purpose of these Standing Stones is not known; they may have been burying places, but some scholars think that they had a meaning as temples for the worship of the sun.

The finest ring of Standing Stones which still survives is the Ring of Brodgar in Stenness. This stands on a low neck of land between the Lochs of Harray and Stenness, and it is remarkably well preserved. There are twenty-seven upright slabs still standing out of a total of sixty and their average height is 7 feet, though one of them is 15 feet high. The smaller circle known as the Standing Stones of Stenness is near by but is not in such a good state of preservation.

The Broch Builders

The megalithic builders of the stone cairns were probably mission-aries who were anxious to spread their religion over as wide an area as possible. The main emphasis in this religion was laid on the burial of the dead and differences of opinion as to how this should be done can be seen in the different shapes of cairns which they erected. For the most part, the peoples who used the cairns probably belonged to the

Neolithic, or New Stone Age, but, after they had settled in Orkney for some time, a Bronze Age people called the Beaker folk arrived from the mainland of Great Britain.

These new invaders may have come originally from Spain or Portugal, and they were interested in trading their bronze wares among peoples who had formerly used clay pots and weapons of bone or stone. They derive their name from the beakers which they introduced, though they have also left behind articles made from copper and gold. Originally, they seem to have preferred to be buried in single graves lined with stone, but some of them may have been converted to megalithic forms of burial. It is thought that they erected the circles of Standing Stones and that Stonehenge in England may be their most enduring monument. It is almost certain that the Beaker folk inter-married with the earlier megalithic settlers, and so a mixed race was produced which was probably more vigorous and progressive than either of the original races from which it was derived. What language was spoken by these early Orcadians will never be known as they left no written records.

Sometime around 200 B.C. or 300 B.C. other invaders came to Orkney and Shetland bringing with them weapons and tools made out of iron. It is difficult to know where these Early Iron Age people came from, but it is certain that they were farmers rather than herdsmen. They are famous as the builders of the *brochs*, or thick-walled circular fortresses, which are to be found in great abundance both in Orkney and in Shetland. The word broch comes from the Old Norse word *borg*, a place of defence, and this would suggest that the brochs were fortifications where the Iron Age farmers could seek shelter when they were attacked by enemies.

The most famous broch in the north is the Broch of Mousa in Shetland. It resembles a lighthouse, tapering slightly towards the top. The height of the tower is over forty feet, the wall measures 50 feet in diameter at the base and 40 feet at the summit, and the fortress was surrounded by a stone wall at a distance of 20 feet.

It is thought that the broch was never roofed over, but some shelter was provided by a circular penthouse roof running around the inside.

The Broch of Mousa is double-walled and between the walls there is a series of stone galleries linked by a stairway which curves upwards towards the top. The flagstone floor of each gallery forms the ceiling of the one below it, and the galleries are lit by small window-gaps on the inner wall only. What purpose these galleries may have served is not known, but it has been suggested that they were used as scaffolding at the time the broch was erected. The stairway certainly allowed defenders to climb to the top of the broch when it was attacked by enemies.

We have taken the Broch of Mousa as an example of a broch fortress as it has survived almost intact down through the ages, but there are a number of very interesting brochs in Orkney which have been excavated or examined in recent years. Some of these are surrounded by the ruins of crude stone huts which were, no doubt, occupied by the broch builders when they were not being attacked by enemies. We can imagine that when the attackers came, the owners of the broch retired within their fortress and tried to hold it against all comers. This would have been an easy task, as few weapons in those early times could have made any impression on such thick and durable walls.

The broch dwellers were well equipped to withstand a prolonged siege. Many of the brochs have wells inside them, and, doubtless, supplies of provisions could have been stored in the stone galleries. The solid stone walls could not have been burned down, and it would have been almost impossible to have forced an entrance through the narrow doorway. Indeed, spears could have been thrust down from the galleries above through gaps left between the roofing stones of the passage.

We have mentioned already that the broch builders were farmers, and this is proved by the many quern stones found on broch sites. Most of the Orkney brochs were near the most fertile lands which still yield the heaviest crops in those particular areas. When the broch folk were not at war, such tasks as the grinding of grain, the cooking of food, the spinning of wool, and the making of clay pots would have been carried on by the women, while the men would have been busy tilling the soil, forging weapons of war, and, perhaps, fishing in the surrounding seas and lochs. Many spinning wheels and weaving-combs have been discovered on broch sites, thus proving that some, at least, of the arts of civilisation were known to these early farmers.

In Orkney, the distribution of brochs raises many interesting questions. Along the Evie shore of Eynhallow Sound there are no less than six brochs, while there is a similar number on the Rousay shore. In Sanday there are brochs on most of the nesses, or peninsulas, and in Burray, the Broch Island, there are three large brochs near the shore. Usually these round fortresses were built near the sea, as though invaders were expected to come from somewhere outside these islands and make an attack. This should not surprise us when we remember that, at the beginning of the Christian era, many tribes were on the move and piratical raids must have been of frequent occurrence in every island community.

The Picts

Many attempts have been made by historians and archaeologists to find out precisely who the broch-folk really were. It is a fact that, in the early years of the Christian era, and for many centuries afterwards, the tribes living in the north of Scotland were called Picts, and many guesses have been made as to where they originated and what language they spoke. The word *Picti*, or 'painted people', was applied to them by the Romans who recognised them as fierce warriors against whose raids on the Lowlands of Scotland it was necessary to build walls. These Picts may have spoken a Celtic language which was the fore-runner of Gaelic, but some ancient inscriptions contain words from an older tongue not yet identified by scholars.

Perhaps the best theory put forward so far is that the Picts were not a separate race at all, but rather a mixture of different races.

Two or three thousand years before the birth of Christ the Stone Age people arrived in the north of Scotland, and, sometime not very long after their arrival, they were joined by Bronze Age Beaker folk who were anxious to sell their wares. Thereafter a series of invasions may have occurred, each invasion bringing a different tribe with new ideas, until finally the Iron Age broch people reached our shores. The fact that the broch people built strong fortresses is an indication that, even with their coming, invasions may not have been over.

Thus, as each set of invaders reached the north of Scotland, it is likely that they did not exterminate the tribes which they found there already, but after a few warlike skirmishes settled down peacefully amongst them either as equals or overlords. Intermarriage between the various tribes would have been common, so that after a lapse of a century or two it would have been difficult to tell who were the descendants of Stone Age settlers, or of Iron Age warriors. It was to this mixture of races that the name *Picts* was applied.

The great burial cairns, the Standing Stones, the village of Skara Brae, and the brochs together form a heritage from Orkney's pre-historic past of which all Orcadians may justly be proud. Their very presence seems to link modern man with his early ancestors in a way unique in Britain. They make us feel that the past is still with us even in this age of tractors, motor cars, and high-speed aircraft.

REFERENCES

F. T. Wainwright, *The Northern Isles*. Nelson, 1962.
Inventory of the Ancient Monuments of Orkney and Shetland, 3 vols. H.M. Stationery Office, 1946.

NORSE INVASION AND RULE

The Early Christian Missionaries

MANY years before the Norse colonisation began, Orkney had already been visited by Christian missionaries. Although it is not known who was the first Apostle of Orkney, Adamnan's *Life of St Columba* tells of an appeal made by that saint to the Pictish king at Inverness on behalf of any monks who might travel to Orkney. The story then refers to a monk called Cormac who visited Orkney and returned safely to Iona. Missionaries from St Ninian's settlement at Whithorn may have come as far north as Orkney, for one feature of the Celtic church was the fondness of its monks for small islands and solitude. Some sailed as far as Iceland before the Norse colonisation of that island began. There were active missionaries in the Celtic church as well as hermits.

As there is little written evidence about the christianisation of the Picts in Orkney we have to use all sources of information. The presence of Christian priests in the islands at the time of the coming of the Norsemen is referred to in a Latin document which is thought to date from the twelfth century. There it is stated that Orkney was at first inhabited by the Picts and Papae. The Papae were the Celtic clergy, and the word survives in the names of the islands Papa Westray and Papa Stronsay. Perhaps there were monastic settlements on these islands. Other centres of early Christian witness are indicated by the names Papdale in Kirkwall, and Paplay in Holm and South Ronaldsay. It is interesting to find in Papa Westray the remains of a chapel dedicated to a Pictish saint Triduana, here called Tredwell.

Other evidences of the early church in Orkney are to be seen in stones with incised crosses of a type which dates from the seventh or eighth centuries. The Pictish symbol stones of which a number have been found in Orkney are characteristic of the Christian period of the history of the Picts. Two small iron bells, of a type common in the Celtic church, have been unearthed, one in Birsay and the other in North Ronaldsay.

The 'Papa' names all apply to fertile places; but on one infertile headland called the Brough of Deerness there is the site of an ancient

THE WEST COAST OF WESTRAY

from the painting by Stanley Cursiter, R.S.A.

Celtic monastery. To approach this from the landward side one descends to the stony beach of a geo,[1] and then climbs by a narrow path up the side of the peninsula called The Brough. The ruins of a small chapel are visible. Under the turf there lie the foundations of about sixteen rectangular buildings, mostly the cells of the monks. It is probable that this monastery was founded as early as the eighth century; it may even date from before 700. Another early church site was on the Brough of Birsay. In 1935 a broken stone slab with Pictish symbols and the figures of three armed men was found on the Brough of Birsay in an ancient burial ground which became the site of a Norse church. To one island the Norsemen gave the name Holy Island— Eynhallow—and remains of a medieval monastery still stand there. The name surely indicates that an important religious settlement was already there when the Norsemen came. There is evidence to show that Christian influence was well diffused through Orkney by the beginning of the eighth century, and there is reason to believe that the Norse conquerors did not long remain pagan.

In the *Orkneyinga Saga*[2] it is told that in the year 995 King Olaf Tryggvason of Norway came to Orkney. He found Earl Sigurd on board a ship off Walls at Osmundwall, and offered him the choice of baptism or death. The earl accepted baptism, and the saga says, 'Then all the Orkneys became Christian.' It is doubtful if Sigurd did much to promote Christianity after this nominal conversion. The saga gives the impression that the Norse inhabitants of Orkney were mostly pagan until 995, but this is unlikely. The evidence of place names, and the continuing reverence for early Christian sites suggest that the Celtic clergy were not exterminated by the Norsemen, and that many of the newcomers and their descendants were gradually won over to the Christian faith. In his *Orkney Farm Names* Dr Hugh Marwick shows how the fairly common name Kirbister provides evidence 'that there were Christian Norsemen living in Orkney long before the official conversion of these isles'.

The Coming of the Norsemen

Viking raids preceded the Norse colonisation of Orkney. By the eighth century the Scandinavian people had attained great skill in the craft of ship-building. Ships from the Viking period which had been preserved for centuries in burial mounds may now be seen at Oslo. Adventurous seamen set out in many directions and made notable voyages of exploration. They colonised Iceland, and ventured beyond

[1] A narrow inlet on the beach.
[2] See p. 10.

2

to found settlements in Greenland and North America. Their descendants the Normans adopted the customs of the French and won for themselves a notable position in western Europe.

There is no record of the first coming of the Vikings to Orkney. At first, doubtless, they made sporadic attacks, carrying off spoil and slaves. One habit of the Vikings was 'ness-taking'. They would settle on a suitable ness which was easily defensible, and make it their base for further raids. But later there came ships carrying men who did not intend to return home with loot, but who came as land-hungry emigrants looking for opportunities in the west which they did not find at home. The foundations of farm-houses dating from an early period of the Norse settlement may be seen on the Brough of Birsay.

The Norse Earls

The *Orkneyinga Saga*, written in Iceland in the thirteenth century, is our main source of information about the history of Orkney from the creation of the earldom towards the end of the ninth century until the beginning of the thirteenth. It is the story of the earls and chieftains, not the story of the people of Orkney. From an early period Shetland and Caithness were included in the earldom. When the earl was a strong man he acted rather as an independent ruler than as a subject of the king of Norway. The period of Scandinavian domination lasted until 1468, but the later earls belonged to Scottish families. Few records have survived from the thirteenth and fourteenth centuries. It is no wonder that the period of the Norse earls, and especially the twelfth century, has been called the Golden Age of our island history.

The first earl, Sigurd the Mighty, is said to have conquered a good part of the north of Scotland. Of one of his successors, Einar, the story is told that he taught the islanders how to cut turf from the bogs for fuel. Einar had to flee for a time when an unruly son of the king of Norway descended on Orkney. This intruder had murdered Einar's father in Norway. The murder was avenged on North Ronaldsay, where the king's son was slain and his body was made an offering to Odin. Not much is told of the seven earls who succeeded Einar. The saga writer is more interested in, or better informed about, Earl Sigurd Hlodver's son[1] and the raven banner which brought victory to the army before which it was borne, but death to the standard-bearer. It was this Sigurd who was suddenly faced by King Olaf with the choice of baptism or death. Sigurd died in battle in Ireland. 'There was no

[1] For an explanation of the use of surnames, see Chapter 9.

man who would bear the raven-standard and the earl bore it himself, and fell there.'

For a time two sons of Sigurd Hlodver's son shared the earldom. Brusi was a peaceable man and a good ruler, but his brother Einar compelled men to leave their farms in summer and go on war-cruises. Their farms suffered, and they got little reward for their war service. This led to the murder of Einar. At this period we read of the holding of *things* or assemblies. Two place-names indicate meeting places of *things*: these are Tingwall in Rendall and Dingishowe in St Andrews. In the *Orkneyinga Saga* the *things* do not have the same importance as they have in other Icelandic sagas.

Earl Thorfinn

Thorfinn Sigurd's son, who succeeded to a share in the earldom as a youth, became a powerful ruler. His military and naval exploits are celebrated in the saga in prose and verse. Arnor Earl's-skald[1] was a close friend of Thorfinn. Many of his verses are quoted. In them the saga writer had contemporary evidence for the events he describes. Writing of the use of such poems, Snorri Sturluson, thirteenth-century author of *Heimskringla*, said, '. . . we find the best evidence in the poems that were recited in the presence of the chiefs themselves or of their sons; we take everything to be true that is found in these poems about their journeys or battles. It was the way of skalds to give most praise to those in whose presence they were reciting; but no one would dare tell the chief himself what he and all the listeners knew to be false and imaginary; that would be mockery, not praise.'

The saga account of the extent of the dominions in Scotland and the Western Isles may be exaggerated; but Thorfinn's rule extended beyond the Norse settlement of Caithness, and he retained his conquests. He became known as Thorfinn the Mighty. The ruthless methods employed in the struggle for power in the eleventh century are illustrated in the story of his feud with his nephew Rognvald Brusi's son. Rognvald had spent some time at the Norwegian court and had seen service in Russia, when he came to Orkney to claim a share in the earldom. After some years of harmony trouble broke out between Thorfinn and Rognvald, and this led to fighting. Rognvald was defeated in a sea battle in the Pentland Firth and escaped to Norway. At the beginning of winter he returned with one ship. The first intimation Thorfinn had of his return was when one night the house where he was staying was set on fire. The women and bondmen were allowed to leave, but no quarter was given to Thorfinn and his bodyguard. It was

[1] Scandinavian poet or bard

thought that he had perished with his men, but with his wife in his arms he managed to jump clear and escaped unseen through the smoke. At the shore he found a boat and rowed over to Caithness. Secure in the belief that Thorfinn was dead, Earl Rognvald went to Papa Stronsay for malt a little before Yule. That evening, as the company sat before a great fire, the house was surrounded. Thorfinn had come. The house was set on fire, and all except the earl's men were permitted to leave. One man who was taken for a priest got out safely and immediately disappeared in the darkness. When the small island was searched, Earl Rognvald was found on the beach, betrayed by the barking of his little dog, and put to death. After Thorfinn had killed thirty of Rognvald's followers he no longer had any rival in Orkney.

The next event in Thorfinn's life shows his courage and shrewdness, and also gives an example of a sense of honour which helped to restrain bloodshed in a barbarous age. Thorfinn knew that King Magnus of Norway might take vengeance on him for the death of his loyal friend and vassal, Rognvald. Thorfinn dealt boldly with this danger. He sailed to Norway, came to where the king's ship lay at anchor, went up to the king where he sat at meat, greeted him, took up a loaf of bread, broke off a piece, and ate it. The king handed his cup to the stranger. Then Thorfinn revealed his identity. The king said, 'It is true, Earl Thorfinn, that I did not mean that if we ever met as we do now thou shouldest be able to tell of our parting. But as things stand now, it ill becomes my honour to have thee put to death.' The king would not take speedy vengeance on a man whom he had just accepted as his guest. Not long after, King Magnus died and Thorfinn was on good terms with the new king, Harald Hardrada.

For the rest of his life the great earl ruled in peace. He made a pilgrimage to Rome. He lived mostly at Birsay and had a church built there called Christ's Kirk, the first cathedral in Orkney. The official guide-book issued by the Ministry of Works identified the ruined church on the Brough of Birsay, long known as St Peter's, with Thorfinn's Christ's Kirk. Remains of other buildings to the east of the church may indicate where Thorfinn had his palace. The saga admits that though he was popular in his own hereditary lands, 'in those lands which he had brought under him by the sword, it seemed to many a hard lot to live under his rule'.

Hakon and Magnus

Two peace-loving men, Paul and Erlend, sons of Thorfinn, were succeeded by their sons, Hakon and Magnus. Hakon Paul's son is described from the first as an overbearing man, whereas Magnus was gentle and pious. The main part of the story of Magnus in the *Orkneyinga Saga* seems to be based not on oral tradition but on a clerical life of the saint. His story is also told in two Magnus-sagas. It may be that the story as we have it exaggerates the villainy of Hakon by contrast with the panegyric on Magnus. Certainly Magnus left a remarkable impression on the minds of the men of his own generation.

While the cousins were still young men, the king of Norway came to Orkney and carried them with him on a war-cruise down the west coast of Scotland. The king led his men in harrying and plundering. They went as far as Anglesey and attacked the ships of two Welsh earls in the Menai Strait, but the young Magnus refused to fight, saying that he had no quarrel with any man there. It is said that he took a psalter and sang while men fought around him. Conscious of the king's anger, Magnus escaped from the ship by night and swam ashore; he seems to have stayed for a time with the king of Scots.

When at last Magnus came home again, Hakon and he each ruled part of Orkney as a grant from the king of Norway. At first there was a good relationship between them, but mischief-makers brought about bad feeling. Well-disposed men among the chiefs tried to bring about a reconciliation. It was agreed that the two earls should meet on Egilsay in Easter week. Each was to have two ships and an agreed number of men. Magnus was the first to arrive. When Hakon came he had several ships and a large force of men. It became clear that there was to be no reconciliation. Magnus made three suggestions. He offered to go on pilgrimage and never come back to Orkney. When this was rejected, he offered himself for imprisonment in Scotland. Hakon and his men again rejected this. Then Magnus gave the third choice—that they should maim him in any way they pleased and put him in a dark dungeon. Hakon was prepared to accept this, but some of his men would not allow it. So Hakon commanded his standard-bearer to kill Magnus. When this man refused, the cook was made to do the deed. After prayer Magnus said to his executioner, 'Stand thou before me, and hew on my head a great wound, for it is not seemly to behead chiefs like thieves. Take good heart, poor wretch, for I have prayed to God for thee, that He be merciful unto thee.'

Earl Magnus was buried at the church which his grandfather had built at Birsay. He began to be revered as a saint and martyr. Stories were told of miraculous cures obtained by men who made pilgrimages to his grave. The saga gives a favourable account of the later years of Earl Hakon. It tells of his journey to Rome and Jerusalem, and of his growing popularity thereafter. It was probably he who built the Round Church, the ruins of which stand in the churchyard of Orphir.

Earl Rognvald

A few years after the death of Earl Hakon, his son Paul was sole ruler of Orkney. His rule was beneficial. Then a young Norwegian put forward a claim to a share in the earldom. He was Kali, son of a sister of Earl Magnus. He demanded half of Orkney as heir to Magnus. Later he adopted the name Rognvald. The king of Norway accepted his claim, and granted him the title of earl. Paul resisted the claim, and Rognvald's first attempt to establish it by force was unsuccessful. Then his father, Kol, said to him, 'Now my advice is to seek for help where it is abundant, for I think that he may grant thee thy realm who had it by right—I mean Saint Magnus the Earl, thy uncle. I desire that, to provide for his granting thee the ancestral lands that are thine and were his, thou make a vow to have a church of stone built in Kirkwall in the Orkneys, when thou gainest that realm, so that there be not a more magnificent in the land; and let it be dedicated to Saint Magnus the Earl thy kinsman.' The vow was made. The saga tells how, partly by guile and partly by a show of force, Rognvald was able to make good his claim. The opposition of Earl Paul came to an abrupt end. One morning he had gone with some men to hunt otters on the shore at Westness in Rousay, when he was kidnapped by that powerful and adventurous man, Sweyn of Gairsay. It was probably in 1137 that the work of building St Magnus Cathedral began.

Earl Rognvald is one of the most interesting characters in the saga. The stories that are told about him, and the verses he composed to suit various occasions, show him as an attractive man with a lively mind. During his expedition to the Mediterranean and on to the Holy Land he appears as an amorous knight, a Viking out for plunder, and a pious pilgrim. St Magnus as depicted in the saga, though spoken of with the highest respect, is a shadowy figure of a man compared with his nephew. Rognvald was murdered in Caithness. The saga pays this tribute to him: 'He was a friend in need to many a man, liberal in money matters, equable in temper, steadfast in friendship, skilful in all feats of strength, and a good skald.' Earl Rognvald the cathedral builder became St Rognvald.

Sweyn of Gairsay

We have already been introduced to Sweyn Asleif's son, of Gairsay, kidnapper of Earl Paul. The first incident told of him in the saga shows him fishing in the Pentland Firth with two men from Swona. In a later

chapter we see him as the farmer of Gairsay, and from his home on
that island, Langskaill, he set out on annual Viking cruises. Sweyn
often saw St Magnus Church on Egilsay, and he must often have passed
the holy island, Eynhallow; but the strongest influences on his career
were those of his pagan forefathers.

Sweyn met his death at the hands of the townsmen of Dublin, who
had determined to put an end to his plundering. In their eyes he was
one of the most unjust of men. Yet he had heroic qualities. J. Storer
Clouston says of him, '. . . for hardihood and endurance there were
few to equal him. It is also certain that he must have had great charm
when he chose to exercise it.'

The saga is largely the story of the earls. Sweyn is prominent because,
though not of the highest rank, he was a man of great influence. The
church of Orkney is represented by Bishop William 'the Old', who
held the see for a remarkably long time. He had a residence in Egilsay.
After the founding of the cathedral he must often have been in
Kirkwall, and may have been the builder of the oldest part of the
bishop's palace there. The endowment of the cathedral by Rognvald
must have strengthened the bishop's position. William accompanied
Earl Rognvald on the expedition to Palestine. One cannot help
wondering what he thought of some of the exploits of his companions.
A successor of William was Bjarni, son of Kolbein the chieftain of
Wyre. Both these bishops were often consulted by the leading men of
the islands. Bjarni was one of the outstanding men of his day in the
north, a poet and diplomatist. In his time the work of building the
cathedral advanced considerably. It was through his influence that
Earl Rognvald was canonised in 1192. Fine churches were erected in
the twelfth century, including those of Egilsay and Orphir. Nothing is
known of the priests who served under the early bishops; but
Rognvald made merry over the sight of sixteen monks at Westray—
in one of his topical verses he made fun of their dress and their bald
heads.

The End of Norse Rule

Orkney was part of the kingdom of Norway until 1468, when it came
under Scottish rule. There is little to tell about the later centuries of
Norse rule, for few records survive from the thirteenth and fourteenth
centuries. After 1232 the earls of Orkney belonged to Scots families,
and Scots influence also came in through many of the bishops.

As the church grew more wealthy its bishops became more powerful.
At least one king of Norway looked on the power of the bishops as a

threat to his own position. One of the conditions agreed to by Henry Sinclair when he received the earldom was that he would 'make no league with the Bishop of Orkney, nor enter into or establish any friendship with him unless with the good pleasure and consent of our said lord the king, but that we assist him against the said bishop until he shall do what of right or deservedly he ought to do in those things which our said lord king desires, or may reasonably demand of the said bishop'. Anyone who wishes to study the story of the church in Orkney in the medieval period and on to the seventeenth century must read Dr Craven's *History of the Church in Orkney*.

In 1263 one of the greatest of the Norwegian kings, Hakon Hakonson, came with a large fleet to Orkney. He was on his way to the west of Scotland with the purpose of asserting his authority over his Hebridean possessions. A few months later he returned to Kirkwall in poor health, having lost many of his ships. He died in the bishop's palace and was buried in the cathedral. The following spring his body was taken to Norway.

Henry Sinclair, the Scots earl mentioned above, built a castle in Kirkwall towards the end of the fourteenth century. It is commemorated in the name Castle Street. The building of the castle was a breach of a promise made by the earl on his installation. He must have felt himself strong enough to risk the displeasure of the Norse king, and he had the king of Scots to turn to. The castle of Kirkwall was a strong fortress, according to the testimony of an earl of Caithness who wrote two centuries later, 'I protest to God the house has never been bigget without the consent of the devil, for it is one of the strongest holds in Britain without fellow.' By the fourteenth century the inhabitants of Orkney had ceased to engage in acts of piracy. In that and the following century there were complaints of raids on Orkney made by Highlanders.

The long period of Norse domination was at an end.

REFERENCES

A. B. Taylor, *Orkneyinga Saga*. A new translation. Oliver & Boyd, 1938.
J. Storer Clouston, *History of Orkney*. Kirkwall, 1932.

3

RETURN TO SCOTLAND

THE transformation of the once powerful and semi-independent earldom of Orkney into a Scottish county was a gradual process. Even before 1468 a certain amount of change had taken place. For more than two centuries the earls of Orkney had been Scottish noblemen, owing fealty to the king of Scotland for Scottish lands, and, for Orkney, to the king of Norway. Several of the bishops, also, had been Scotsmen, though subject to the archbishopric of Trondheim. Inevitably these earls and bishops brought from Scotland relations and friends who settled in Orkney and made their homes there. Changes in the system of land tenure were already creeping in, and the feudal system was beginning to make itself felt. Even so, Orkney in 1468 was still Scandinavian.

In Norway, as well as in Orkney, changes had taken place since the great days of the sagas. All three Scandinavian countries were now under the dominion of the king of Denmark, who in 1468 was King Christian I. Between King Christian and the Scottish king relations were unfriendly, chiefly because of the non-payment of the tribute called 'The Annual of Norway'. In 1266, three years after the battle of Largs, King Magnus of Norway had handed over the Hebrides and the Isle of Man to Scotland on promise of payment of an annual sum of money for all time. The bargain had not been kept, the Scots had defaulted, and King Christian tried to force a settlement. The king of France was called in as arbitrator, and after much negotiation a marriage was arranged between the young king of Scots—James III —and Margaret, King Christian's daughter, who was to receive a dowry of 60,000 Rhenish florins. Ten thousand florins were to be paid at once, and for the balance the rights of the Danish king in Orkney were pledged until the debt should be paid. The debt has never been paid, and Orkney remains Scottish.

Transfer of the Earldom

By this arrangement the rights of the Danish king, and the laws, law-courts, and system of land tenure of Orkney were safeguarded. All too soon, however, Earl William Sinclair—the last hereditary earl of Orkney—was constrained to hand over to the king his earldom, in exchange for the much less valuable estate of Ravenscraig in Fife. Thus the king of Scotland became earl of Orkney, and in 1471 the Scottish parliament annexed the islands to the Scottish crown, on condition that they should not be given away except to a lawful son of the king. In 1472 the bishopric also passed from Norway, and was placed under the archbishop of St Andrews.

The new earl—the king—being naturally unable to live in Orkney, granted a lease of his new estates to the bishop, William Tulloch, who, for a fixed sum, collected the rents and skats due to the king.

Such leases—or tacks—were henceforward common in Orkney, and were a great source of discontent because often the holder of the lease used his power unscrupulously. Bishop William, for instance, drew all the tithes and rents of the church as well as of the earldom emoluments, and the great power which this gave him enabled him to extend church holdings at the expense of the earl's, for earldom and church property were so intermixed in the parishes of Orkney that it was easy for the bishop to manipulate affairs to his own and the church's advantage. Bishop Andrew, William's successor, held the tack until 1489, when it was given, along with the office of Justice, to Henry, Lord Sinclair, grandson of the last Sinclair earl. This was a good and popular appointment, for the Sinclair earls understood Orcadians, and were liked by them. Unfortunately for Orkney, Lord Henry, along with his king and many another, was killed at the disastrous battle of Flodden. The tack of Orkney remained in the hands of Lord Henry's widow, but the office of Justice was entrusted to Sir William Sinclair of Warsetter, on whose death the young son of Henry, Lord William Sinclair, was, through his mother's influence, made Justice Depute of Orkney. His high-handed behaviour quickly led to trouble, and a rebellion broke out under the leadership of James and Edward Sinclair, sons of Sir William of Warsetter. The udallers of Orkney, fearing further encroachments of feudalism, enthusiastically supported the brothers. The castle of Kirkwall was taken and Lord William was forced to flee.

The Battle of Summerdale

The ejection of the king's deputy—Lord William—could not be tolerated; King James V appointed the earl of Caithness—also a Sinclair—to assist Lord William in crushing the rebellion. An army was raised and in 1529 across the Pentland Firth it sailed to Orkney. Landing on the Orphir coast, it proceeded by a devious route towards Kirkwall. At Summerdale, on the borders of Stenness and Orphir, it was met by the Orcadians under the Sinclair brothers and was totally defeated. The earl of Caithness and many more were killed; the residue were captured or driven into the sea. Earl William was among the captives. Later he was set free and returned to Scotland.

Visit of James V

The victory of Summerdale was the last pitched battle fought in Orkney. It was a decisive victory, for the rebels, instead of being punished, were forgiven, and in 1535 their leader, James Sinclair, was made a knight. Perhaps the king was impressed by the strength of the rebellion; or it may be that he and his advisers feared that, if driven too far, the islanders might return to their Scandinavian allegiance. Whatever the reason, the rebels escaped punishment, and in 1540 the king himself paid a visit to Orkney and was entertained royally by the bishop.

Earlier, in 1468, James III had made Kirkwall a royal burgh, and had affirmed its ownership of the cathedral of St Magnus. His charter was now confirmed by his grandson, James V. The office of Justice, however, he abolished, instituting instead a Sheriff—and thus bringing nearer the absorption of Orkney into the political pattern of Scotland.

Upon the king's death in 1542, after the ignominious defeat of Solway Moss, the queen mother, Mary of Guise, claimed the earldom, with its rights and emoluments, as her dower. A Frenchman, Bonot, appointed by her, was governor and sheriff in 1558, but little is known of this period of confusion in Orkney.

The Reformation

In the momentous year 1560 the queen mother died; and the Reformation took place in Scotland. At this time Adam Bothwell was bishop in Orkney. His diplomatic and tactful manipulation of affairs and individuals in the islands ensured that an event which violently convulsed many parts of Scotland passed in Orkney without incident. The clergy for the most part conformed to the new religion and stayed in their parishes. Many of them married. As for the people, they were either obedient to their priests—or were not easily moved to religious enthusiasm. In truth, the general behaviour of the clergymen of Orkney before the Reformation was not such as to encourage true religious fervour in their parishioners.

The year 1560 marked also another development in the feudalisation of Orkney; this was the formation of very large feudal estates from the lands of the church and the earldom. These estates were held by Scotsmen—not by native udallers.

The queen of Scots, Mary, had by this time returned to her native land. Generous as she always was to the illegitimate sons of her father, she gave a grant of Orkney—along with the sheriffdom—to her half-brother, Robert Stewart, in 1564, a very unfortunate appointment for these islands. He was, indeed, temporarily deprived of his power in 1567, when Mary made her third husband, Bothwell, duke of Orkney. After the defeat of Carberry Hill the new-made duke fled to his new estates; but his one-time supporters there, Bishop Bothwell and Gilbert Balfour, governor of the castle, both turned against him and drove him from the islands. Again Orkney was left to the tender mercies of Robert Stewart.

To describe in full the evils which Earl Robert inflicted on the hapless Orcadians would be almost impossible; we shall mention only a few. Skat or rent was always paid in kind, and the old Norse weights and measures were used to assess the amount payable; the earl altered these, so that the tenants were cheated and impoverished; people were imprisoned—even executed—without trial; dead men were tried, for real or trumped-up offences, and their goods or estates confiscated; the free intercourse of ships across the Pentland Firth was stopped, lest some voyager should carry the story of oppression to the authorities in the south. Free people were forced to labour for the earl without pay, as though they were serfs or slaves. The old udal laws and institutions were twisted and altered to suit the earl's selfish purposes. The udallers were practically ruined, and their lands confiscated and given out under feudal law to Scottish hangers-on of the earl.

Earl Patrick Stewart

Earl Robert's death in 1591 did nothing to relieve the tortured earldom, for his son Patrick, who succeeded him as earl, though much less able than his father, and far less astute, was equally tyrannical. One of the main complaints against him was that he made laws to suit his own purposes, and then pronounced sentence on his unfortunate victims according to the laws he himself had made. He is credited with the destruction of the ancient Law-book of Orkney; he destroyed the Records of Kirkwall, and tried to reduce its status to that of a burgh of barony. The Orcadians were worse off than under his father, for they suffered the same and additional oppressions, and they were poorer. Their circumstances were indeed intolerable, but a deliverer was at hand.

The church in Scotland had had a chequered history since the establishment of Presbyterianism in 1560. In 1573 bishops were restored, though so much were they under the dominion of the nobles that in derision they were nicknamed 'Tulchan'—or stuffed calf-skin —bishops. In 1592 Presbyterianism had its turn, but in 1606 the king, James VI, feeling strong enough after his accession to the throne of England to assert himself, restored episcopal rule. Of this time Dr Craven says: 'The state of vital religion in Orkney was at a low ebb. Profaneness, error, superstition, neglect abounded. A firm hand was needed.'

The deliverer with the 'firm hand' was James Law, the new bishop, a friend and favourite of the king. When the bishop discovered the appalling condition of affairs in both church and earldom, he set himself, with patience and skill, to put matters right. In 1608 he sent a most diplomatic letter to King James, laying before him in such moving terms the distresses of the poor people of Orkney that in 1609 the earl was arrested and imprisoned in Edinburgh Castle. Through the influence of friends, and the reluctance of the king to punish him, he might still have escaped punishment but for the vigilance of the bishop and his own foolish arrogance. He prevailed on his natural son, Robert, a young man of twenty, to raise on his behalf a rebellion in Orkney. Robert was for a time surprisingly successful; but the appearance on the scene of the earl of Caithness—burning to avenge Summerdale—as the king's deputy, and the treachery of one Patrick Halcro, brought complete defeat to the unfortunate young man. In January 1615 he was hanged in Edinburgh, and in the following February his father was there beheaded. Thus ended the rule of the Stewart earls.

The death of the earl did not rid Orkney of all its troubles. The earl of Caithness, if not prevented by the bishop, would have destroyed the cathedral. Nor did the bishop's good offices end there. He did his best to bring order into church and state. To solve the confusion between church and earldom properties, all the church lands were surrendered to the crown, and then certain whole parishes were allocated by the king to the church. This happened in 1614. The bishop was empowered also to appoint sheriffs and bailies to be his own officials—independent of the civil officials. Again the earldom was annexed inalienably to the crown, and matters seemed at last to be settled.

In 1638, however, the scene altered once more, with the renewed expulsion of the bishops from the Scottish church, and the ensuing Bishops' Wars. No doubt Orkney would have been as indifferent to this upheaval as it had been to the other vicissitudes of the church but for the appearance in the islands of the 'Great Marquis'—Montrose. In 1650 Montrose, in the hope of gaining support for the king in his struggle with parliament, sent emissaries—and some soldiers and equipment—to Orkney from the Continent. It is likely that they were received with little enthusiasm: yet when Montrose himself landed in Kirkwall he found that his messengers had succeeded in recruiting about one thousand islanders. With these and 500 German and Danish mercenaries he crossed the Pentland Firth to Caithness, but he met opposition and open hostility. Marching south by the coast road he halted at Carbisdale, near Invershin, where his troops were surprised, dispersed, and cut down by a detachment of Scots cavalry. Montrose and several of his principal officers were captured and executed in Edinburgh. Few of the islanders, other than a garrison which had been left in Caithness, survived this desperate venture.

Orkney did not escape further punishment. General Leslie sent a contingent of soldiers, who ravaged the country and quartered themselves on the inhabitants. Then, in 1651, Cromwell sent an occupying army to the islands. The earl of Morton, to whose father in 1643 Charles I had leased the earldom, was driven out. A fort was built on the north side of Kirkwall, and Cromwell's soldiers ruled in Orkney until the Restoration. On the whole, the Cromwellian rule seems to have been better than any since 1468. According to Tudor the English taught the Orcadians many useful things, such as improved methods of agriculture, weaving, and the use of the spinning-wheel. Many of them married Orcadian wives, and some even settled in Orkney. Above all, their methods of dispensing justice seem to have been fairer than any that the islands had endured under Scottish rule.

The year 1660 brought an end to the Cromwellian inter-regnum. The earl of Morton returned and blamed the Kirkwall magistrates for destroying his seats in the cathedral; but for that they blamed the 'Englishes'. In 1669 the islands were again annexed to the crown, and by act of parliament made into a Stewartry; again they were leased out to 'tax farmers', whose main aim was to exploit the islands for their own gain.

The church became once more Episcopalian—a change which the Orcadians accepted, as they were to accept the final change to Presbyterianism thirty years later, with complete equanimity. During the whole period under review the church, whichever one was in power, exercised the strictest church discipline. Offenders were summoned before the church authorities, and were forced to do penance by standing at the church door, in sackcloth, on Sundays. If they had any money they might be allowed to pay a fine instead. There is little reason to think that morals were improved by this harsh treatment. Indeed one commentator avers that the notoriety of doing penance was actually enjoyed by some. One of the most cruel and useless manifestations of church discipline was the witch-hunting that was carried on in Orkney, as it was in all Europe in those days.

We have now reached the end of the seventeenth century. The udal system of landholding had disappeared, never to return. The greatest landholders were now Scotsmen, many of whom had bought their estates with money gained by trading, chiefly with Norway; for Norway was glad to exchange timber, sorely needed in Orkney, for the grain which the merchants had obtained by buying the rent and skat paid in kind to the earl or holder of the tack. Agriculture was in a very backward state. Fishing on a commercial basis was unknown; if a man fished, it was for his and his family's use. Education was enjoyed only by a few, for the only schools we hear of were the 'Sang School', established in Roman Catholic times for teaching boys to take part in the cathedral services, and the grammar school in Kirkwall. The latter had been long in existence; we hear from time to time how the bishops appointed teachers for the schools; but we know really little about them, and only a select few could have been educated. All in all, the people of Orkney must have been both impoverished and miserable. Considering the oppressions they had had to suffer, and the penalties and humiliations they had endured, the wonder is that they had any spirit left in them.

REFERENCES

B. H. Hossack, *Kirkwall in the Orkneys*. Kirkwall, 1900.
J. R. Tudor, *The Orkneys and Shetland*. London, 1883.

4

AGE OF STAGNATION

WHEN we try to see what Orkney looked like for most of the two hundred years before our own twentieth century we almost feel as if we were looking through the wrong end of a telescope, for everything is a little smaller. Kirkwall is just a long straggling street and Stromness a village. Finstown and Dounby do not exist. In the country there are hardly any houses with a second storey. The fields are so small that they are little more than cultivated patches. Even the animals—horses, cows, pigs, and sheep—are a good deal smaller than those on our farms today. But there are a surprising number of those old-fashioned animals, and they seem to swarm over the hillsides, hungrily eating the rough herbage.

We are used to looking out over great stretches of cultivated land, especially in places like the West Mainland, so that we hardly know where farms begin and end, or where parishes meet. Our great-great-grandfathers saw a very different Orkney, farmed haphazardly and containing far greater areas of natural pasture and moorland.

The parishes all existed as they do now, and as they have done for a very long time. There was a parish minister. There should have been a parish school, although more often there was not. There was a laird, who owned a lot of the land; or even several lairds. But few of them lived for long periods in their native parishes. Life was more interesting for them somewhere else. The ordinary people for the most part spent their whole life in the parish, and were proud to be known as a Deerness man or an Orphir man, or whatever the parish was. But they took many of their surnames from districts that were once far more important than parishes. These districts were called *toonships*.

Toonships

Surnames like Isbister, Hourston, Groundwater, Marwick, Corrigall, and a lot of others are toonship names. Toonships were areas of good, easily farmed land, which had been in use for centuries, perhaps even before the Norsemen came to Orkney. They varied in size according to the amount of useful land, and were situated wherever the good land had been found: along the shore or the loch, in a fertile valley

Prehistoric settlement at Skara Brae

Hut interior—Skara Brae

Maeshowe, a chambered cairn

The Ring of Brodgar

drained by a burn, or perhaps on a hillside facing to the sun. One thing they had in common—a boundary wall of turf and stones which separated them from the waste land outside. There would be quite a number of toonships in a parish, some adjacent, others with a good distance between them.

In some of the toonships, especially in Harray, the old Norse families had been so strong and firmly rooted in their land that the Scottish tyrants, of whom we have already read in this book, could not displace them. These lived in what were practically family toonships. At the beginning of the eighteenth century some of them were still speaking the old Norn[1] language; and, as their land was divided equally among their children according to the udal law of Norway which Orkney had inherited, without any need of papers to give them possession or to prove this and that, they were called *udallers*.

In the greater part of Orkney, however, udallers had almost ceased to exist. Other people had managed to get large portions of the toonships; sometimes because they were powerful, and related to the important Scottish families who now ruled the islands, or because they had money enough to buy the land from impoverished udallers. There were places, especially in the good, easily cultivated North Isles like Stronsay and Sanday, where the toonships were already broken up and large farms were making their appearance.

With it all, however, the way of life in the toonships was characteristic of Orkney right into the nineteenth century. Within the toonship was the very best land called the *toomal*, the not-so-good land, and some pasture land. Everyone owned a part of the toomal in one piece, but their land in other parts of the toonship was divided into tiny little fields, scattered all over the place. This was so that their owners had equal shares of good land and poor land; but from the farming point of view it was a great nuisance. The narrow fields were drained by the earth being heaped up in ridges or *rigs*, and the method of farming was called *runrig*.

The Farm

As there were no fences, cultivation could not be attempted in spring until the hordes of animals which had spent the winter roaming over the toonship, and making a hideous mess of the fields, had been sent outside to spend the summer on the moors and hills. Before this took place the dyke around the toonship was heightened and strengthened; but, even so, animals were always finding their way back and being chased out again by rough, yelping dogs. There were gates in the dyke

---

[1] Norn—the Norse dialect formerly spoken in Orkney.

so that travellers could pass through, and these had to be carefully closed. The gates were called *slaps* or *grinds*. The latter word lives here and there in Orkney farm names.

The Orkney farmer in the eighteenth century had a hard time, and he was an obstinate person. Because his way of farming was a poor one the land did not grow a great deal, but he firmly believed that it would be fatal to alter his methods. He grew oats and bere year about, had never seen turnips, and would only manure his land with seaweed. The plough he used was much the same as people had in Old Testament days. He threshed his crop with a staff, hinged by leather to a handle, which was called a *flail*; and he ground his corn between round quern stones, such as are sometimes seen today ornamenting gardens.

Because the land was so poorly worked few people depended on it entirely for a living, or if they did they were often in sore straits. Some of the better-off lairds had ships with which they carried cargoes to and from Norway or the Baltic ports. They might take away meal, fish, rabbit skins, feathers, and tallow; and they might bring back sugar, tea, spices, calico, brandy, and gunpowder. The lairds also introduced *kelp-burning* to Orkney. All the spring, on suitable shores, people would carry up seaweed to be dried and burned. The residue that was left when the seaweed was burned produced iodine and other chemicals, as well as soda which was used for making glass, and the profit from kelp-burning was considerable. It was in the eighteenth century, too, that cod and herring fishing first became important to Orkney. These employments helped to keep people alive, but they prevented them from making full use of the land, which we now know is so rich and valuable.

In the kitchen the women worked at spinning and knitting, and, at a slightly later date, helped with the making of linen, for most of the clothes that people wore were made in their own homes or toonships. Men's jerseys and women's petticoats, for instance, were knitted at home; but the cloth for making into jackets, skirts, and trousers was manufactured by weavers, of which each parish had at least one, and sometimes two or three. The weavers occasionally built their own looms, and they worked very hard, but neither they nor the tailors were much thought of by the women of the parish, possibly because their crafts were considered to be too 'womanish' for a proper man.

The Farmhouse

There was little comfort in an eighteenth-century Orkney house. It was most often a tiny place, built with stones and clay and roofed with thatch or flagstones. It seldom had more than two rooms, lit by small windows, or sometimes by skylights only. The fire was built against a low wall of stone in the middle of the room, and the smoke found its way out through a hole in the roof. The cattle lived in a byre which was only partly detached from the living-room. Human beings and animals often entered the house by the same door. It has been thought that the original reason for this was that the warmth of the cattle circulated through the house in winter and kept the temperature fairly high. No-one objected to things being rather messy, and sometimes pigs and hens were allowed to snuggle up against the wall where the fire was built. The furniture was simple. There would be a stool or two, a table, and a heather basket, or *kaisie*, for the peats. In the early days the bed was in a stone recess filled with straw, which was built as a lean-to against the back wall; but box-beds later came into general use. Rough cupboards built into the walls were used for storing food and clothes. Some houses were even more poorly furnished than this, while others were slightly more comfortable.

With life as hard as it was in the old days in Orkney no one was inclined to fuss over food. There were times, right up to the nineteenth century, when crops were so poor that people faced famine and frequently died of starvation. Landlords who had a store of meal would dole it out in small quantities, and people would walk miles to get a share. When things grew very bad the government sent meal to the islands to keep people alive. Pork, mutton and dried fish, bannocks, kail and brose, birds' eggs and shellfish—all washed down with water or ale, were the food of the eighteenth-century Orkneyman. By the end of that century he had added potatoes and turnips to his diet; and the coming of potatoes meant that people could grow them in quantity and were never so desperately hungry again. Everyone drank great quantities of ale because tea was scarce and dear, and because the cattle were so starved during the winter that they gave little milk. Indeed there were still in the early nineteenth century over a hundred ale-houses in Orkney.

As a rule folk did not travel a great deal around Orkney, for they either had to walk, or ride one of the native horses, or get a boat to take them between the islands. Those who were working for other people seldom got a holiday, and few could afford to take a journey for pleasure. The roads were merely narrow tracks between parish and parish. Loads were carried along these by strings of pack-horses. Carts came later; and at last coaches and gigs. The sea was used a great deal as a highway, and there were far more boats in Orkney than there are now.

Piracy, Murder, and Rebellion

It may sound as if Orkneymen lived a quiet, uneventful kind of life, and in a way that is true. But there was always something happening that people got excited about. There were pirates on the seas, and ships were sometimes captured by them. One Stromness boy, John Gow, grew up to be a notorious pirate. He came home to Orkney in 1725, and among other misdeeds plundered the house of Clestrain in Orphir. Then he sailed north in his ship the *Revenge*, but was unlucky enough to run aground on the Calf of Eday, where at last he was captured by James Fea of Whitehall, who owned Carrick in Eday. James Fea handed Gow and his crew to the authorities, and the pirate and some of his associates were executed in London. In that very same year of 1725 one of Orkney's most distinguished naval officers, Captain James Moodie, was murdered on Broad Street, Kirkwall, during a quarrel with the Stewarts of Burray. He died from a shot fired by a servant.

Both James Fea and Sir James Stewart of Burray came into the Orkney news again in 1745, when they and some other Jacobite lairds gave aid and sympathy to the Young Pretender, romantically known in Scotland as Bonnie Prince Charlie. After Culloden, Fea had a mansion at Sound in Shapinsay burned by the Hanoverian troops—one of several lairds' houses in the North Isles to suffer this fate—and Sir James Stewart was captured by a son of the murdered Captain Moodie and sent to Southwark Gaol, where he died. It did not end there, for the Moodies' own home at Melsetter was twice sacked by Caithness Jacobites in 1746.

Smuggling and Whalehunts

If the lairds had their wild adventures, so also had the common folk. In most of the parishes there were people who lived by stealing sheep. They sometimes even dared to sell the stolen sheep to butchers in the towns, although the penalty for their offence could be execution or banishment. The risks they ran gave sheep thieves something of the glamour in Orkney that highwaymen had in England. Even more people took part in smuggling, an activity to which nearly everyone was sympathetic. French and Dutch luggers came frequently to Orkney— indeed almost to the end of the nineteenth century—bringing with them brandy and tobacco. When night fell, boats would slip out from sheltered bays all over the islands and return with contraband cargoes. These cargoes were stored in little-known caves, or even brought to Kirkwall, where there were safe hiding places in many an old house. Preventive officers who were sent to Orkney to stop smuggling could seldom get people to talk. There are traditional stories which suggest that more than one of them got killed in encounters with smugglers.

Men and boys found vent for their fierce energies also in the whale hunts, which took place whenever a school of whales got near to Orkney. In fleets of little boats they drove the whales ashore, brandishing knives, harpoons, and pitchforks, and shouting wildly in their excitement. The capture of a large number of whales meant that money would come into a district, for whale-oil and whalebone were in great demand. A whale chase sometimes made an island richer by £300 or more.

Old Ideas and Customs

Possibly the more timid Orcadians felt a shudder run down their spines when they heard stories of smugglers and sheep thieves; but there were other beings of which everyone, young and old, were certainly afraid. These were not humans, but uncanny creatures who were supposed to live in the sea and among the hills. It is difficult for us to remember that no one then knew what was inside mounds like Maeshowe, or in the *knowes*, as they were called, which covered brochs like Gurness and Midhowe. It was thought that these green mounds were the homes of fairies—not pleasant story-book fairies, but rather dangerous ones—and people gave them a wide berth, especially at night. In the sea, sailors thought they had seen great monsters, one of which was called *Teran*, and also half-human creatures like seal-men and mermaids. The beings who were supposed to live in the hills were called *trows*. They were ugly and ungainly, but they had magic powers, and could be friendly enough unless you angered them.

Some people were scared as well of old men and women who happened to be odd and cantankerous. These were shunned because they might be witches, or possess the *evil eye*. If you got on the wrong side of one of them you were liable, folks said, to become sick or queer; or your fields might no longer grow corn, your cattle might die, or your hens refuse to lay. To protect themselves from supernatural beings and witches people used what were called *charms*. They would go through a process of strange actions, reciting rigmaroles of old words or rhymes. When they were sick they would swallow the nastiest mixtures of stuff which were not really medicines, but which were thought to be useful in combating the evil influences which had caused the illness. Before the Reformation there were lots of little chapels all over Orkney dedicated to one saint or another. These had fallen into ruins, but many Orcadians still believed that the saints after which the chapels were named had wonderful powers, and when they were in difficulty they went to pray in the ruins, or to leave money in them, so that the saint would help them. The Scottish ministers, who now preached the reformed religion in Orkney, tried very hard to do away with the old beliefs and superstitions, but they were not very successful.

It must not be thought, as some have done, that because Orkney people in earlier centuries were very poor, sometimes hungry, and occasionally frightened of hard masters and supernatural powers, they had no fun in life. They were often merry, as the comical and high-spirited stories they have left behind them most certainly show. They were great story-tellers. Nothing pleased them more than to sit by the fire on a winter evening remembering the old legends, or trying to see who could spin the most ridiculous yarn. Besides, they had their own adventures on land and sea to recall, and old songs to sing. There were special songs for special tasks. One helped the milk to churn more easily; another relieved the tedium of spinning, and seemed to make the wheel go faster.

They liked to build bonfires at Beltane (the beginning of summer), or better still at Johnsmas (midsummer). The whole population of a district gathered round the fires, capering and dancing. If you seized a burning brand from the fire and ran with it all the way around a field or a house, then it was believed that the field would be fruitful, and everyone inside the house safe and prosperous.

When there was food enough, and the proper occasion, feasts were held. The occasion might be a wedding, the end of harvest, the season of Yule, or the New Year. Because people liked the feasts so much they would sometimes last for days. No one minded where they slept: if there was straw in the barn or a temporary bed on the floor, they were entirely happy. The great holiday in the islands was Lammas, at the beginning of August. From all over Orkney folk gathered at Kirkwall, to meet each other, make merry, buy necessities for the winter, and to listen to, and laugh at, the cheap-jacks who had their booths in front of the cathedral.

Even if Orkney could be pleasant, however, in its easy-going old-world way, it was very far from being the kind of place that far-sighted Orcadians wished to see, and there were reformers here and there with ideas about the future. How the islands began to change into the Orkney we know, we must read in the next chapter.

5

THE BEGINNINGS OF
MODERN ORKNEY

ALTHOUGH many interesting things happened to Orkney in the nineteenth century, the most important of them all was the change which
took place in farming. Because the farmers were persuaded at last to
try new methods, Orkney slowly became a county of green and fruitful
fields. We owe so much to this revolution on the farms, to which is due
the easier and pleasanter life we live today, that we ought to know how
it took place. But before we read about the making of the new farms,
we must look at what was happening at the beginning of the nineteenth
century.

The Wars with France

Agriculture was then poorly understood in Orkney. We have seen
how badly the land was cultivated, and how people neglected their
farms for kelp-burning and fishing. But it was not always of their own
choice that men left the land for other jobs. Because Britain was at war
with France men were required for the navy. Hundreds of Orkneymen
served in Nelson's ships, some of them playing their part in great sea
battles like Trafalgar. A proportion of these men may have volunteered
to serve, but others had been caught and forced to enlist by the
press-gang.

It was the press-gang's task to capture men for the fleet. Because it
was difficult to persuade men to accept the sometimes brutal conditions
on the men-o'-war, the government had to take them by force. Whenever the constables of the press-gang were known to be in the county,
nearly every able-bodied man in Orkney found himself a hiding place,
perhaps in a cave, or in a hole below the floor, or in a hollowed-out
peat stack. There were many exciting chases, and some clever escapes,
but a lot of men were captured.

Each spring as many as fifty whaling ships came to Stromness, where
they engaged hundreds of Orkneymen to go north to Greenland as
seamen and harpooners. Other men went to Canada with the Hudson's
Bay Company to become labourers and fishermen and traders. These
men were called *nor-wasters*, and although many of them came home
again after five or ten years a considerable number settled down in

Canada. These sent home orders to Stromness for much of the clothing, tools, and other articles they needed; and that town, which had by now grown a good deal bigger, was getting prosperous through trading and provisioning ships.

The Need for Improvement

With two thousand men, or perhaps even more, working outside Orkney when they ought to have been at home cultivating their farms, things were in a sorry state. Many a little farm had no man on it to do the work, so women did ploughing, harrowing, and sowing as best they could. Where there were big properties the landlords tried to keep the men at home; but the cultivation of areas composed of very small properties for a time grew even worse than before. People often had to live on the money that their sons and daughters could manage to send them.

The only people who could help Orkney were the large owners of land, of whom there were not a great number, for nearly three-quarters of Orkney was swallowed up in a dozen or so big estates. The most important of these properties was that which had once been the earldom estate, but which now belonged to Lord Dundas. Most of the tenants to whom the farms on the larger estates were let were content to carry on in the old-fashioned way, for they had neither the capital to bring about reforms nor leases of long enough duration to ensure that they would benefit from their labours. As for the landlords they had other interests; and while trading, fishing, and kelp-burning helped to keep up their revenues it was hardly to be expected that they would tackle the very difficult task of turning the Orkney lands, divided into thousands of tiny patches by the old system, into modern farms. The people of Orkney were against this. Landlords who tried to reform their estates were sadly disliked.

The First Steps

Nevertheless, even before the nineteenth century, small experiments in modern farming had been tried. Around 1760 one or two Kirkwall merchants became the owners of lands in Stronsay, which they tried to improve with a good measure of success. Before the end of the eighteenth century Stronsay had an agricultural society, the first in Orkney. In other islands—particularly in Burray, at the Bu—improved methods were being introduced. It was in the 1760s also that an attempt was made to destroy the runrig system, and to divide the land into fields; but the fields were so tiny, and still so intermingled, that little good came of it.

It may be that the wars in which Britain was engaged during the latter part of the eighteenth century, and the first decade or two of the nineteenth, impeded farming; for they made fishing in safe Orkney waters important, and increased the value of kelp, which rose from 45s a ton to £20 a ton. When peace came after Waterloo things began to change. Kelp in less than fifteen years became almost unsaleable. Orkney's linen and straw-plait industries were in decline. Men came back from the navy looking for work. There was nothing left but the land.

New Methods and Ideas

Things were not easy for the landlords, many of whom had been brought to the brink of ruin by the depression in trade which followed the war, and by the failure of the kelp industry. But their only option was to improve their estates or give them up. Almost to a man they set to work, with new ideas from farther south to guide them. A lead came from the owner of the earldom estate, who began to grant leases, and made his tenants follow a series of *Regulations*, which included a proper rotation of crops. Some proprietors had anticipated in a small way this example, others now began to follow it. They were helped by a series of *plankings* (dividing the land into fields) which began in the 1830s, and which continued for the next thirty years. The fields were now of reasonable size, out of which real farms could be made.

To bring the new farms into being a lot of things had to be done. The proprietors had to divide the land into holdings of various sizes, with new buildings and enclosures. They had to remove people from impossibly small crofts in the way of the improvements and find them somewhere else to live. They had to choose tenants who were willing to farm in the modern way. They had to bring in new and better breeds of cattle, horses, and sheep. They had to replace old implements like hooks and flails with reaping machines and threshing mills, or at least persuade their tenants to do so. And, most unpopular of all, they had to get permission to divide up the common land, which everyone had used for their geese and sheep for generation after generation.

Not all the improvements could be made without hardship. Some landlords were kind, and went to much trouble to see that people were not left homeless and helpless. Others carried through their reforms with less humanity, leaving a reputation for severity which is still remembered in the Orkney parishes. On the whole they relied on example. They engaged experienced farmers from the south to be the managers of their home farms, and brought others to Orkney as tenants. Although this policy was resented, its wisdom gradually became clear.

It is obvious now that the rents were too high; and people living in poverty were angered when they saw fine new mansions going up on the big estates. Although landlords had to pay heavy duties, the worst of which was known as *superior duty*, they doubtless passed on a proportion of the burden to their tenants.

When the new farms were made a lot of people were elbowed out. It was customary for these to be given twenty or thirty acres of waste land, which they cultivated with great toil, working early and late to reclaim their land. They made drains and built houses, creating from almost nothing the fertile little crofts which sprang up around the older farms.

It is astonishing how quickly agriculture began to flourish once the improvements were well under way. Owing to conflicting estimates we are unable to say quite how much arable land there was in Orkney when the improvements began, but there was at least two and a half times as much by the end of the century. The new breeds of cattle were far more valuable. By 1866 they sold for twice as much as they had in 1850, and four times as many were exported. The rise in the export of sheep was greater still. But the hen outstripped all competitors: from a hundred thousand dozen eggs sent out of Orkney in 1833 the figure mounted to one and a half million dozen by 1895. With the prosperity of the land increasing so quickly more people stayed at home; and this, with better conditions of health, brought the population of the islands to over 32,000, in 1861.

Transport

We must not forget that great changes were also taking place over the whole of Great Britain, and that Orkney shared in the general improvement. For instance, the provision of well-made roads made it much easier to take goods to and from the markets; and the coming of the steam-ship, plying first between Orkney and the south, and later between our own islands, opened up trade in a completely new way. With mail coaches rattling along the road to Stromness, with a steamer taking people to Kirkwall from the North Isles, and with hotels and public buildings being erected in both towns, Orkney felt that it was joining in the march of civilisation. It got its own newspapers, the *Orcadian* and the *Orkney Herald*; and from the printing presses came the first truly native Orkney books, the best of them all a book by the Sanday farmer, Walter Traill Dennison, entitled *The Orcadian Sketch Book*. With prosperity came more time for cultivating leisure, and some Orcadians turned with great zeal to natural history and archaeology.

Education

It was a time of revolution, in the good sense. People wanted better schools, and got them. Church people in Orkney felt that they had been too easy-going. So new denominations sprang up, with plenty of energy and zeal. The reformers were not always wise, but they were good for Orkney, which needed to wake up from centuries of slumber. It seemed that everything had happened at once. There was a sense of pioneering excitement in Orkney last century which must have made it an interesting place to live in. It is always a good sign when people begin to make poems about their own country, as a number of Orcadians had begun to do, even if they are not very good ones. And it is a good sign when a country has men to spare to explore foreign lands. Orkney had these as well, for John Rae explored large parts of the frozen north of Canada, and William Balfour Baikie did valuable pioneering work in Nigeria.

Trade

When money begins to come in to an area which has been very poor, lots of things begin to happen. People begin to improve their homes, they buy things they fancy, and even their food begins to change. The Orkney houses that we are familiar with today may be for the most part neither big nor grand, but very many of those substantial slate-roofed farmhouses we see around us were built last century and replaced mere huts and hovels. People bought, or made, furniture to put in their new homes. With more money in hand they got a taste for refined food; which may have been a pity, for oatmeal and beremeal gave place to flour. Few fruits could be grown, but rhubarb flourished like a weed in most gardens, and cupboards full of jars of rhubarb jam might almost be noted as a distinguishing mark of Orkney life. The demand for different food, and for a host of other things, encouraged trade. If we look around Kirkwall and Stromness we shall see that the majority of the bigger businesses sprang up from the middle of last century onwards. The merchants, who had once been content to wait until people came to them, now went out to bring their goods to the people. Travelling shops, loaded with all types of articles from cakes to paraffin, could be seen on most Orkney roads; and one enterprising firm fitted out a series of little ships as 'floating shops', which traded with islands and remote communities in Orkney, Shetland, and the north of Scotland.

The Crofters' Charter

Well before the end of the nineteenth century, Orcadians, apart from unfortunate people here and there, may be said to have achieved freedom from want. But there were other freedoms which, like people elsewhere in Britain, they were denied. We have noted that the land itself belonged largely to big proprietors. For the privilege of living on that land the ordinary small farmer or crofter had to pay dearly. He had to pay a rent, not necessarily in money but in grain, malt, butter, and so on; he often had to meet ancient taxes over and above his rent; and, in addition, he had to work at the busy periods of sowing, hay-making, and harvest on the landlord's own farms. Until 1889, when county councils came into being, the ordinary Orkneyman had little say in the running of the islands. The county's business was carried on by a body of people called Commissioners of Supply. You could not be a Commissioner unless the yearly rental of the land you owned was over £100 (Scots). In practice these local rulers were the big landlords and their friends. We do not find that in the main they were tyrants, but we can understand what it felt like to be a crofter whose voice did not count for anything in Orkney affairs.

By far the greatest grievances of the crofters were the size of their rents and the fact that they could be turned out of their homes when the landlord wished. They could never feel secure. There were many hundreds of such people in Orkney. On some estates they were treated honourably, but on a few the threat of eviction was always hanging over their heads. This applied to crofters in other parts of Scotland as well. It had been felt for a long time that the whole system was unfair and that the crofters should be protected by law. Many years passed before parliament was willing to take action, but at last it came, with the Crofters Holdings (Scotland) Act of 1886. This for the rank and file of the Orkney people was probably the greatest event of the century . . . the Act has been called 'The Crofters' Magna Carta'.

From now on—those who framed the Act were saying—crofters must have fair rents and conditions, and they must be secure from eviction. In 1888 the persons appointed as the Crofters Commission came to Orkney to see that the changes which were necessary were carried out. Their coming had been eagerly awaited. They sat for the first time in Stromness Town Hall on the 14th of August. The hall was full, and the windows had to be opened so that people outside could hear. An Orkney lawyer, Mr Thomson, made a fine and moving speech on the crofters' behalf, then the business began. From the Mainland the Commission went to the islands. Day by day crofters were interviewed and their grievances heard. Most landlords acted with fairness and dignity when they were questioned. But the plight of the crofters had not been exaggerated; rents were greatly reduced, and much of the arrears of rent due to the landlords was cancelled altogether.

The time had come when the crofters of Orkney could regard their little holdings as homes in which they could live securely, and which their children could inherit. This meant, however, that the landlords were sometimes hardly hit, especially if their incomes came mainly from their estates. These two factors, the increased security of the crofters and the growing insecurity of the landlords, between them set the stage for many of the great changes of the twentieth century.

6

TWENTIETH-CENTURY ORKNEY

In Orkney the twentieth century began quietly with little indication on the surface of the ferment of new ideas which was at work. The full effect of the 1886 Crofters' Act was now beginning to be felt, and with the security of tenure at fair rents which it ensured, farmers were prepared to make improvements to their holdings and to practise new methods of agriculture. It was now worth-while to do so. A similar measure passed in 1911 strengthened the Act by raising the rental qualification from £30 to £50 a year. The more important changes which were to turn Orkney into a county of owner-occupiers were not yet apparent, and in the meantime the road to betterment for many ambitious young men still lay across the sea. It was not only the Pentland Firth which they crossed to Scotland or England, but the great oceans of the world to Canada, the United States, Australia, and New Zealand.

An indication that Orkney's insularity was no longer absolute came by accident on a stormy night in December, 1910, when two Germans knocked at the door of Park Cottage, on the outskirts of Kirkwall, and asked what country they were in. On the afternoon of the previous day they had set out from Munich in a balloon, intending to stay aloft overnight and to land perhaps in Switzerland. With a change of weather and a rising wind, they were carried across Europe and out over the North Sea before they realised what was happening. Hope was receding when in the darkness of their second night aloft, thirty hours after leaving Munich, they saw the lights of Kirkwall and made a successful landing. It was the first time that Orkney had been reached by man without the use of a boat—the dawn of island air travel.

The First World War

The Great War came to the islands without warning. As early as 1812 Scapa Flow had been recommended to the Admiralty as a fine natural anchorage, and units of the fleet had made frequent summer visits. But when the navy was ordered north by Winston Churchill in the last days of July, 1914, it came to a war station which was quite unprotected but ideally placed to block any movement of German shipping through the North Sea to the Atlantic. It was to be used in two World Wars, though to a lesser degree in the second, and it was to bring a great influx of soldiers, sailors, and airmen into the close community of the islands. Now heavy coast-defence guns were hastily mounted and manned by Orkney's volunteer soldiers of the Territorial Army, Royal Garrison Artillery, at the main entrances to the Flow, and old ships were sunk across other channels to deny the anchorage to enemy submarines. Later, mines and boom nets were put down and for four long years the great ships of the Grand Fleet had a secure base under the dark hills of Hoy. In 1916 the fleet sailed from Scapa under Admiral Jellicoe to engage the German High Seas Fleet at Jutland, an indecisive battle which both sides claimed as a victory. British losses were considerable, but the German fleet never put to sea again until 1918, when it came to Scapa under the guard of British guns to be interned.

It was in the summer of 1916, too, that the cruiser H.M.S. *Hampshire* went down three miles off Marwick Head in Birsay. On board was our greatest army commander, Lord Kitchener of Khartoum, then Secretary of State for War, who was on his way to Russia. He embarked in Scapa Flow on the *Hampshire* which set out in a rising summer gale on a course west of Orkney. Off Birsay the cruiser struck a mine and sank with the loss of almost the entire ship's company. It was an event which moved the British people deeply for Kitchener's name was a household word.

There was tragedy again in the Flow the following year when the battleship *Vanguard* mysteriously blew up while lying at anchor, again with the loss of almost everyone on board.

Meantime, during these years of war, thousands of young Orcadians had left the islands, or had returned with the Colonial forces, to serve in France, the Near East, and on the seas, many with distinction. When fighting ceased in November 1918, nearly six hundred had given their lives.

The German Navy

The naval base now held not only a British fleet but the disarmed German navy as well. Manned by skeleton crews these great ships lay sullenly at their moorings through the winter of 1918–19 while the victorious Allies debated their future. The German sailors solved the problem. On 21 June, 1919 they jammed open the seacocks, the ships filled, heeled over, and sank. Seventy-four warships began to rust at the bottom of the Flow.

They were too valuable to remain undisturbed for long. In 1924 there began an astonishing feat of salvage which provided work for many Orkneymen in the lean years between the two wars. Within little over a year from the beginning of the operation the firm of Cox and Danks had raised many of the sunken destroyers, but few people thought that the great battleships, 700 feet long and 90 feet beam, would come to the surface again. Though the difficulties were great and the work was dirty, cold, and dangerous, new salvage techniques were developed and one by one the German boats were refloated—*Moltke*, *Seydlitz*, *Kaiser*, *Von der Tann*, *Hindenburg*. Finally in the summer of 1939 the *Derflinger* was brought up and beached in Rysa Sound where it remained until the Second World War was over. Then in 1947 it was towed south to be broken up, as the others had been in the earlier years.

From Crofter to Owner-occupier

As the country returned to a peace-time economy after the Great War, the landowners in Orkney found that the rates on their property, together with stipend payable to the church, and other duties (such as skat, the old Norse tax which was still levied on many farms), absorbed most of the rents fixed by the Crofters' Commission thirty years before. So from 1920 onwards they began to break up their estates, selling the holdings in most cases to the sitting tenant. Usually these tenants were able to buy their farms and crofts at the equivalent of twenty to twenty-five years of the gross rent of the place and the landlord made a fairly good deal on the transaction. On the other side, the rents were low and the houses and buildings on the crofts and farms already belonged to the tenant, so that when he became the owner of the land the actual sum of money which he had to pay over was not so big as to be a burden to him. He still faced great difficulties. Just after the war the prices for farm produce, especially for grain, fell sharply. Quick to adjust his economy to changing conditions, however, the Orkney farmer switched from trying to sell oats, which dropped from 62s a quarter to 22s in one year, and instead fed the grain to poultry. The marketing of eggs, which had long been a profitable sideline, now became a major item in the business for many years. At its peak over 70 million eggs were exported annually, bringing in a gross income of about £1¼ million. Recently costs have increased, marketing conditions have become less favourable, and the industry has declined.

The main effort of the island farmer for over a hundred years has been to increase the area and productivity of his arable land. It was possible to increase the area since most small farms included heath land and the process of reclamation began as far back as the mid-nineteenth century. Arable ground, from a figure of 72,000 acres in 1870, was

The Broch of Gurness at Aikerness
Round church at Orphir

The St Ola *sailing past Hoy*

Marwick Head and the Kitchener Memorial

increased acre by acre to over 90,000 by 1939, that is, at least 18,000 acres of previously useless land were brought into a condition suitable for the growing of crops. By this time all the dry hill on many farms had been reclaimed, but a fresh impetus to further development was given in 1940 when government grants became available to help the work, and at a later date the Department of Agriculture gave further practical assistance by providing on hire excavators and ploughing outfits. It has therefore been possible since the Second War to undertake more ambitious projects and larger areas, so that within this period about 11,000 acres, an annual average of 700 acres, have been brought into cultivation. Though increased area is not the only factor, the progress made by the industry during this century is shown by the following figures of stock in the county:

Year	No. of cattle	No. of sheep
1900	28,054	35,789
1959	56,542	88,039

Land reclamation is seen to be a successful long-term policy, which will no doubt be continued until many more thousands of acres have been turned over.

Highland Airways

The great story of the development of air travel is a part of world history of the years following the Great War, and within that period the main air routes over the continents and oceans were mapped out. At one time it seemed likely that Orkney might be part of a transatlantic air link, but the increasing range of aircraft made this unnecessary. Then, in the thirties, a pilot of much experience, Captain E. E. Fresson, flew north and began to show the advantages of connecting isolated communities, especially those separated by sea, by means of aircraft. In 1933 he opened up a regular service between Inverness and Kirkwall, using a twin-engined seven-seater biplane. The public response was immediate and enthusiastic, for he cut a journey of twelve uncomfortable hours by boat and train to a mere seventy minutes' flying time. Orcadians became the most air-minded people in Britain. Soon his company, Highland Airways, was bringing the daily newspapers to Kirkwall, and in 1934 he was given a contract to carry mail—the first internal air-mail service in Britain. In the final stage of Captain Fresson's work the people of the North Isles co-operated with him to prepare suitable landing sites, so that he was able to establish an inter-island service which brought North Ronaldsay within twenty-five minutes of Kirkwall but which was stopped on the outbreak of war. After the war Orkney was included in the network of British European Airways.

The Second World War

Over this scene of progress and relative prosperity—for the economic slump of 1929 and the early thirties did not hit Orkney so hard as it did the industrial areas—there crept the shadow of war with Nazi Germany, and from 1938 the naval base of Scapa became a centre of activity. When the fleet sailed north a year later, the main entrances to the Flow had been put into a state of defence and the minor channels blocked, but not so effectively as to prevent a great disaster. At high tide, on the night of 14 October, 1939, a German submarine found a passage between Holm and Lamb Holm into the Flow. Fortunately most of the Home Fleet was at sea, but the battleship *Royal Oak* was lying at anchor under the cliffs of Gaitnip, an easy target. Hit by several torpedoes the great vessel sank rapidly, with the loss of more than eight hundred men. The submarine escaped undetected.

Soon after this blow the Germans attacked again, this time from the air. Little damage was done apart from the effect of a near miss on the First War battleship *Iron Duke*. One bomber was shot down in Hoy by an anti-aircraft battery manned by Orkney and Caithness territorials.

The navy dispersed to other bases until the defences of Scapa Flow were strengthened, returning early in 1940. During our ill-fated Norwegian campaign which followed the invasion of that country by Germany, much of the naval effort was directed from Orkney. The German bombers came back but were now met by a very heavy barrage of bursting shells: attacks were ineffective and soon ceased.

The disaster to the *Royal Oak* set in motion a plan to build causeways linking four islands to the Orkney mainland and thus blocking the eastern approaches to the Flow through which the German submarine had crept. These causeways bear the name of 'The Churchill Barriers', for Sir Winston Churchill, then First Lord of the Admiralty, was sponsor of this project. The work was carried out in part by Italian prisoners of war who had been captured in North Africa, and it formed a base for the road which now joins Burray and South Ronaldsay to the main island.

From 1941 the war moved away from Orkney, though the navy continued to make limited use of the Flow and large numbers of army and air force men were stationed for a time in the county. Four aerodromes were built, one of which, Grimsetter, is now the civil airport for Kirkwall. Also retained for peacetime use is the radar station at Netherbutton in Holm, which once gave warning of enemy bombers but which now transmits television and radio programmes for the BBC. For Scapa Flow no place in modern defence strategy is seen, and when the naval base of Lyness was closed in 1957 many people who had been employed there had to leave the islands in search of work.

The Modern Community

In Orkney, as elsewhere, recovery after the Second War was slow, but the twenty years which have passed have been a period of continuous development. Leaders in this improvement have been the officers of the North of Scotland College of Agriculture, who have provided expert advice on all farm matters, including the planning of steadings. The most obvious change, regretted by the older men, has been the disappearance of the horse, for so long the pride and faithful friend of the farm. In 1939 there were still 6,250 horses in the islands; by 1960 there were only 718 and more than half of these were ponies. New tractors and implements could do the field work in a fraction of the time formerly necessary, and by that same year of 1960 there were 1,800 tractors on the land, or about one for every ten of the population. The rise in the number of cars brought to the county is even more spectacular:

	1947	1964
Cars	1,183	3,886
Motor cycles	503	379
Goods vehicles	339	736

Agriculture, distribution, and transport are all fully mechanised.

Until recently the lack of local authority services has made it difficult to equip dwelling houses up to modern standards. The first important step was made by the North of Scotland Hydro-electric Board immediately after the war, when they proceeded to cover the Orkney mainland with a network of supply lines so that within a few years most houses had electric light. This was followed by extensive water schemes planned by the county council. Work on the Mainland has been largely completed and the development of a similar service for the islands is now proceeding. Each island is of course a fresh area and requires individual planning and supply. After a halt of several years the Hydro Board has now extended power by underwater cable to Shapinsay and Rousay. The advent of water and electricity is continuing to transform the countryside as modern houses and well-planned steadings rise on the ancient sites.

There is, too, a changed outlook in education. Until 1947 secondary education was only for the minority who attended Kirkwall Grammar School and Stromness Academy, but the raising of the school leaving age to fifteen in that year made necessary wider provision and more attention to practical activities and to the arts. An ambitious scheme of building in both the isles and the Mainland has helped to make the laborious business of learning a pleasant one for young Orcadians, while new aspects of the educational service have also been vigorously developed—the family book service of the county library, a rural cinema circuit, and a community centre in most districts.

Twice within this century the islands have been closely involved in great events of history. Now perhaps the Orcadians look forward only to the freedom of a peripheral county, but they face the future with confidence in their assets of land and sea.

7

POPULATION STATISTICS

The Trend of Population 1755-1961

THE population figures for Orkney, derived from various counts taken during the past two centuries (and adjusted as necessary), are given below; and the trend of population is shown in the diagram.

Time	No. of people	Time	No. of people
1755	23,381	1871	31,256
circa 1793	23,654	1881	31,882
1801	24,445	1891	30,244
1811	23,238	1901	27,763
1821	26,979	1911	25,791
1831	28,847	1921	23,933
1841	30,451	1931	21,993
1851	31,318	1951	21,173
1861	32,225	1961	18,650

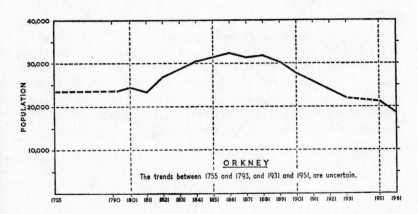

ORKNEY

The trends between 1755 and 1793, and 1931 and 1951, are uncertain.

FIG. 1 The rise and fall of the population over the last two hundred years.

About the year 1755 Dr Alexander Webster persuaded the parish ministers throughout Scotland to count the people. The population of Orkney found in this way was 23,381. Some forty years later Sir John Sinclair, also with the aid of the ministers, showed that around 1793 the number was much the same at 23,654. The official Census Reports, beginning in 1801, continue the story. After 1811 the population increased rapidly, and the upward movement was maintained for fifty years, until the maximum figure of 32,225 was reached in 1861. A significant change presently occurred. In 1871 the population was down; and though a slight increase was recorded in 1881 the decline that followed has continued without a break for eighty years. By 1961 the population was reduced to 18,650.

The rise of population in Orkney was due to a large *natural increase* (an excess in the number of births over the number of deaths)—offset partly by emigration; the fall has taken place because the loss by emigration became greater than the natural increase.

The number of inhabitants is now far below the level of the late-eighteenth century and less than three-fifths of the maximum. For every 100 persons in Orkney in 1861 there were in 1961 only 58. In the fifties and sixties of last century the islands were teeming with life compared with today; and signs of this, in the form of ruined and deserted houses, are visible far and wide.

It is important that we see these changes in perspective. The population trend in Orkney is not unique. A rapid increase during the early decades of the nineteenth century, followed by heavy depopulation lasting into the mid-twentieth century, has been the experience in many outlying regions of Scotland—including counties in the north, the West Highlands, and parts of the Borders. Compared with Orkney, where 58 persons are left out of every 100 in the past, Shetland has retained 55 per 100, Sutherland 52, and Berwick 61. The great increase which has taken place in the population of Scotland as a whole has been due mostly to large increases in the counties of the central industrial belt.

The Mainland Parishes

The following table shows the population of the thirteen parishes which comprise the Mainland of Orkney: (1) at the time of the maximum (along with the date) and (2) in 1961. The last column gives the number left in 1961 out of every 100 in the maximum. The array of parishes runs broadly from north so south and from west to east.

Mainland Parishes	Date of maximum	Maximum population	1961 population	Remaining out of 100
Birsay	1861	1,774	839	47
Sandwick	1861	1,225	832	68
Stromness (including burgh) .	1821	2,944	1,930	66
Harray	1861	819	560	68
Stenness	1861	709	392	55
Evie	1841	907	430	47
Rendall	1851	548	301	55
Firth (including Holm of Grimbister)	1871	789	513	65
Orphir	1851	1,133	507	45
Kirkwall and St Ola (including burgh)	1961	5,672	5,672	100
Holm	1881	1,042	578	55
St Andrews	1851	926	464	50
Deerness	1881	862	395	46

The great tide of population which passed over Orkney last century reached different parishes at different times: the subsequent decline has existed much longer in some than in others. In Stromness parish the highest figure was attained 140 years ago, in 1821; in Evie the time was 1841; other parishes had their maxima later; Holm and Deerness went on growing till 1881. The situation in Kirkwall and St Ola is exceptional: the highest figure was not recorded till the present decade, in 1961. Leaving this parish aside, we observe from the table that Sandwick, Stromness, Harray, and Firth have come off best, retaining two-thirds of their former complement (65 to 68 per 100). In the remoter parishes of Birsay, Evie, and Deerness, however, and in Orphir, less than half the bygone numbers remain (45 to 47 per 100). The most populous rural parishes today are Birsay and Sandwick, and the least populous is Rendall.

The North Isles

Statistics on the same lines are presented below for the North Isles and, in the next section, for the South Isles.

	Date of maximum	Maximum population	1961 population	Remaining out of 100
Outer North Isles				
North Ronaldsay . . .	1881	547	161	29
Sanday	1881	2,075	670	32
Papa Westray . . .	1861	392	139	35
Westray	1881	2,190	871	40
Eday	1851	947	198	21
North Fara	1871	83	0	—
Stronsay	1871	1,267	497	39
Papa Stronsay . . .	1871	32	0	—
Linga Holm	1851	7	0	—
Auskerry (lighthouse) . .	1901	9	3	—
Inner North Isles				
Rousay	1841	976	237	24
Egilsay	1831	228	54	24
Eynhallow	1841	26	0	—
Wyre	1841	96	47	—
Gairsay	1821	79	0	—
Shapinsay	1881	974	416	43
Helliar Holm (lighthouse) .	1931	8	5	—

In the notes that follow, the figures for lighthouses, having little significance, are disregarded. It will be seen from the dates of maximum population, ranging over a period of sixty years, that the decline started in the inner North Isles and spread later to the outer group. The loss of population has been severe. Even in Wyre and Shapinsay, where the fall has been proportionally smallest, less than half the former population remain; in Rousay and Egilsay only a quarter of the people are left; and in Eday only a fifth. Islands that have ceased to be inhabited are North Fara, Gairsay, Papa Stronsay, Auskerry (in 1961), Eynhallow, and Linga Holm. The two last-named have been deserted for more than a hundred years.

The South Isles

	Date of maximum	Maximum population	1961 population	Remaining out of 100
Western South Isles				
Graemsay	1851	286	51	18
Hoy	1851	1,555	506	33
Cava	1861	29	0	—
South Fara	1891	76	5	—
Flotta	1881	425	123	29
Eastern South Isles				
Copinsay (now lighthouse only)	1931	25	3	—
Lamb Holm	1851	13	0	—
Burray	1881	685	262	38
Hunda	1861	9	0	—
South Ronaldsay . . .	1841	2,580	980	38
Swona	1841	54	3	—
Muckle (Pentland) Skerry (lighthouse)	1861	19	3	—
Sule Skerry (lighthouse— 37 miles west of Orkney) .	1931	6	3	—

South of the Mainland the islands that show the smallest proportional losses are South Ronaldsay and Burray, but less than two-fifths of their maximum numbers remain. Since the building of the Churchill causeways during the 1939–45 war these islands (with Lamb Holm and Glimps Holm) have virtually formed part of the Mainland. The island of Hoy, which contains the scattered communities of Rackwick, North Hoy, and Walls, has only a third of its population left; and Graemsay has about a fifth. (It should be noted that the peak figure for Graemsay in 1851 includes various strangers, engaged in constructing the lighthouses.) A few people still remain in South Fara and Swona, but Cava, Hunda, and Lamb Holm have been abandoned.

Sule Skerry with its lighthouse, far out in the Atlantic, is part of the county of Orkney.

The Burghs of Kirkwall and Stromness

The population figures for Kirkwall and Stromness at each census from 1821 onwards (adjusted as necessary) are given below. The trends are shown in the diagram below.

Time	Kirkwall	Stromness[1]
1821	2,590?	2,236
1831	3,065	2,182
1841	3,041	2,057
1851	3,331	2,039
1861	3,525	1,807
1871	3,436	1,626
1881	3,925	1,705
1891	3,900	1,649
1901	3,667	1,750
1911	3,809	1,603
1921	3,692	1,635
1931	3,506	1,560
1951	4,312	1,482
1961	4,293	1,414

[1] Stromness burgh boundary was extended in 1914 and again in 1963.

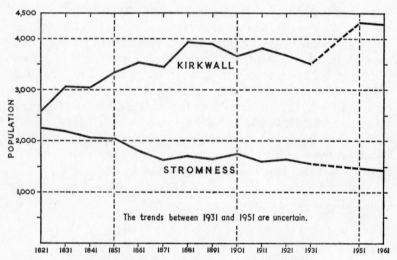

FIG. 2 This diagram shows the divergence in the population trends of Kirkwall and Stromness.

The population trends in the two towns diverge widely. In Stromness there has been a general downward movement, from the peak of 2,236 in 1821 to 1,414 in 1961—with a period of stability from 1871 to 1911. Kirkwall was somewhat larger than Stromness in 1821, having a population (slightly in question) of 2,590. The general trend in Kirkwall has been upward, with a substantial increase between 1821 and 1881, a subsequent decline, and again a marked increase between 1931 and 1951 to the maximum of 4,312. The 1961 population is slightly less; but it is three times that of Stromness, and accounts for nearly a quarter of the inhabitants of the county. So great has been the movement into Kirkwall and its environs that almost a third of the population of Orkney (30 per cent in 1961) are now resident in Kirkwall and St Ola. There are more people in this parish today than in all the North Isles and South Isles put together.

The Loss by Emigration

The statistics of emigration from Orkney during the past hundred years have been computed, and the results are shown below. The figures represent the *net emigration*, by which is meant the excess of *emigrants* over the comparatively small number of *immigrants*. The term *emigrants*, as used here, embraces all persons who departed from the Orkneys, irrespective of where they went. The statistics are approximate.

Intercensal period	Net emigration
1861–1871	4,190
1871–1881	2,460
1881–1891	4,260
1891–1901	4,010
1901–1911	2,870
1911–1921	2,280
1921–1931	1,890
1931–1951 [1]	1,370
1951–1961	2,700

The loss through outward migration has been continuous for many decades and was often heavy. Between 1861 and 1901 the net emigration in a ten-year period amounted at different times to 4,000 or over —an average of more than 400 every year. The total for the past century is around 26,000, nearly half as much again as the present population.

[1] A twenty-year period: there was no census in 1941.

For many years, when the inhabitants of Orkney were too numerous to prosper by the natural resources of the islands, emigration brought a measure of relief; but its momentum has been too great, and now its effect is to reduce the population too far.

Conclusion

The losses of population have been much more severe in the islands than in the Mainland. In 1961 the outer North Isles had 35 per cent left of their former population, the inner North Isles had 33 per cent, the western South Isles 30 per cent, and the eastern South Isles 38 per cent; whilst the Mainland, excluding the burghs, had 65 per cent left, Stromness burgh had 63 per cent, and Kirkwall burgh practically 100 per cent—its maximum was attained in 1951.

The broad pattern of depopulation is plain. The losses are heavier where the lines of communication and transport are longer, and where social and economic conditions are harder.

The outlook ahead is obscure. Further losses must be expected for some time; but it is possible that, eventually, the worth of the natural assets of the Orkneys will hold and sustain a smaller and more settled population, and that an era of stability will come. An increase of population might yet take place.

8

THE PLACE NAMES OF ORKNEY

NOTHING in Orkney is more Norwegian than its place-names. There are probably well over ten thousand of them. Perhaps a score of them are of Celtic origin and a few are Scottish imports. But all the rest were first used by Norwegian settlers and their descendants in Orkney, and most of them still sound as if they were.

The Norwegians who came to Orkney during World War II noticed this at once.

The reason for all this is of course that place-names, if used for a century or two, have an uncanny habit of sticking fast for many centuries afterwards. Their spelling may change from time to time, but they often retain their local pronunciation with very little change at all.

Furse—*a name that has not changed much*

Over forty years ago a schoolboy from Kirkwall Grammar School was on holiday in Rousay and was invited to tea at the farm which appears on the map as Furse. After tea—which is vividly remembered as including three duck's eggs—he went out with the farmer to see his calves, and noticed, almost at the back door, a small waterfall tumbling down over a steep bank into a duckpond. Eager to air his grammar school learning, he explained that this must have been the waterfall that gave the farm its name, because **fors** was the Old Norse word for 'waterfall'. 'This is just what we call it—**Force**,' said the farmer; and —to complete the story—he said that he had never known the meaning of the name of his farm before.

The schoolboy (who is now the writer of this chapter) was also interested to find that, although the map had **Furse**, the farmer's pronunciation was more like that of the name given by the Norsemen eight hundred years before.

Kirkwall—*a name affected by sound-changes*

The name **Kirkwall** has had a more varied history. In Old Norse speech it was **Kirkjuvágr**, 'Kirk-bay'. It appears first in *Orkneyinga Saga* for events about 1140. The saga says: 'At that time the market town of **Kirkjuvágr** had few houses.' (The 'Kirk' was not the cathedral but possibly an earlier church dedicated to Saint Olaf.)

Later forms of the name are many, and here are four that tell their own story:

Kyrkewa 1274   Chronicle of Man.

Kirkwaw 1422   In a legal document printed in *Records of the Earldom of Orkney*.

Kirkwall 1536   James V's charter to the burgh.

Kirkwaa   Nineteenth century—the 1422 pronunciation still used by some of the native 'Kirkwaa' people.

Orkney

The history of the name **Orkney** can be shown like this:

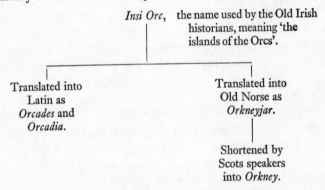

Insi Orc, the name used by the Old Irish historians, meaning 'the islands of the Orcs'.

Translated into Latin as *Orcades* and *Orcadia*.

Translated into Old Norse as *Orkneyjar*.

Shortened by Scots speakers into *Orkney*.

The **Orcs** and the **Cats** were the names of two Pictish tribes. **Orc** meant 'a wild boar'; it is like **porc** without the 'p'. The **Cats** lived in Caithness and gave their name to it. The **Orcs** lived in Orkney and Shetland, and also seem to have left their name in places like the farm of Ork in Shapinsay and a cliff called 'de Orka' in Unst.

The Norwegian settlers in Orkney also gave Maeshowe the name of **Orkahaugr**, 'the mound of the Orcs'. One of them scratched this name in the runic alphabet on a stone inside the mound, where it can be read today. There is thus not much doubt about the name of the people whom Norsemen found in the islands when they first arrived in their long-ships.

The North and South Isles

Here is a glossary of the larger North and South Isles. The map form is given first, then the Old Norse form from the thirteenth century, and then a note on the meaning. We begin with the easy ones:

Sanday	O.N. Sandey	'Sand-island'
Westray	Vestrey	'West island'
Papa	Papey	'island of the papar or monks'
Eday	Perhaps Eithey	'island of the eith or isthmus'
Rousay	Hrólfsey	'Hrolf's island'
Eynhallow	Eyin helga	'Holy Island'
Gairsay	Gáreksey	'Garek's island'
Wyre	Vígr	'a spearhead'
Shapinsay	Hjalpandisey	'Hjalpandi's island'
Hoy	Háey	'High island'
S. Ronaldsay	Rognvaldsey	'Rognvald's island'
Flotta	Flatey	'Flat island'
Burra	Borgarey	'Broch-island'
Graemsay	Grímsey	'Grim's island'
Swona	Svíney	'Swine-island'

All these names make sense. Westray was no doubt so named by early settlers in North Ronaldsay. Eday has an isthmus across the middle. Papa Westray, Papa Stronsay, and Eynhallow have traces of monastic dwellings.

The following present special problems:

Egilsay: O.N. Egilsey. This looks like 'Egil's island', but perhaps Egils was an early Norseman's way of pronouncing the Celtic word *eaglais*, 'a church'.

Stronsay: O.N. Strjónsey. The first syllable may mean 'a place good for fishing' or 'a place good for farming', but we cannot be sure.

N. Ronaldsay: The traditional local pronunciation is Rinnalsay, so it is not derived from Rognvald like S. Ronaldsay. The sagas usually have Rinansey, but three or four times Rinarsey and once Rinalsey. We must label this name 'obscure'.

Three Mainland Names

To Orkney people 'the Mainland' is their own Mainland, not the Scottish mainland, which is 'the Sooth'. They have never used the name Pomona which appears on some maps—just as people in the Western Isles never speak of the Hebrides. Dr Hugh Marwick (*Orkney*, p. 197) explains how the Latin word pomona, 'fruits', in a medieval manuscript of the geographer Solinus was read by someone as if it had a capital 'P'. It found its way into George Lily's map of Britain in 1546, and we have never quite been able to get rid of it.

The parish of Holm is a little puzzling. It is pronounced **Ham**, which comes from O.N. **hofn**, 'a harbour'. Perhaps the spelling Holm comes from the neighbouring island of Glimpsholm.

Birsay must have been, not the present parish, but the island now called the Brough of Birsay. In Old Norse it was **Byrgisey**, 'the island of the fortified enclosure'.

A Walk along the Cliffs

A walk along a line of cliff-tops with someone who knows the local names can be very interesting. We may imagine starting at the Moul Head of Deerness. O.N. **múli** meant 'a snout'. Smaller headlands farther south are White Fowl Nevi from O.N. **nef**, 'nose'; Marki-Ber, from O.N., meaning 'Boundary-rock'. Every deep fissure in the cliff-edge, to be skirted warily, is a **geo**, pronounced 'gyo', and a survival of O.N. **gjá**.

This coast has one of the few 'gloups' in Orkney—O.N. **gljúfr**. This is a deep fissure with a bridge of rock still connecting the sides at the seaward edge. Far below the sea rumbles into the chasm and is sucked out again.

Down to the Shore

When we scramble down to the shore we are almost sure to pass a **naust**, the exact O.N. name for a hollow dug out of the sea-bank in which to beach a boat. We walk round a sandy headland—a **tangi** or Taing. We come to the broad estuary of a stream—an **óss** or Oyce. We turn inland and cross a muddy stretch with **leir** in its name. Lerwick was 'muddy-bay'. We clamber over a **mel** or sandbank, past a **kelda** or spring, and make for a farm called Brecks because it is on a **brekka** or slope.

Up the Hill

The hill might be High Fea in Harray, or Swarta Fiold in Rousay, the second element being O.N. **fjall**, which southerners can recognise in the **Fells** of Cumberland.

High up the hillside there is a sandstone crag jutting out, for which the Norseman's name **Hammar** is still used. We cross a ridge—a **kamb** or Kame—and in a hollow higher up we find a small loch. **Tjörn** was its name, but it has become, not **tarn** as in Cumberland, but **shun**.

There is Loomashun in Rousay, 'the tarn of the red-throated diver'. There were still red-throated divers at Loomashun in our grandfathers' days. Birds and place-names cling to the same spots down the centuries.

The Italian Chapel at Lamb Holm

The Hindenburg refloated in Scapa Flow

An aerial view of Kirkwall

Farm Names

As Dr Marwick showed in his *Orkney Farm-Names*, these names are a study by themselves.

Each name usually contains an element meaning 'farm', and this element gives us an inkling of when it was first settled. Among the older farms, some of them perhaps a thousand years old, are those ending in

-land—Redland, Holland, Trumland
-garth—Midgarth, Nistigar
-bister, O.N. bólstathr—Kirbister, Grimbister
-skaill, O.N. skáli—Skaill, Langskaill

In the early days of the Norse earldom a big farm with a number of small ones grouped round it was given the name bú, and there are farms still called 'The Bu' in many parishes. Later came farms with a man's name followed by stathir, which now survives as ston— Tormiston, 'the farm of Thormothr'; Colston, 'the farm of Kol'.

At a still later stage, stretches of grazing land were fenced off into a kví or quoy, and we have names like Quoyberstane, 'the quoy near the farm of Berstane'. The ending in the farms Cursetter, Melsetter, and Ingsetter also probably means that they were originally grazing land, and not so old as farms ending in ston.

This chapter tells only a little about the history of the Orkney place-names. There is much more information in the three books mentioned below.

REFERENCES

Hugh Marwick, *The Place Names of Rousay*. Kirkwall, 1947.
Hugh Marwick, *Orkney*. Robert Hale Ltd., 1951.
Hugh Marwick, *Orkney Farm-Names*. Kirkwall, 1952.

9

PERSONAL NAMES IN ORKNEY

IN a small primitive community it is possible to get along with just one name. But if one particular name became rather popular—if there were too many Johns—then people were driven to distinguishing them by other means. One John was given a nickname, another was described by the name of his father or mother, a third by where he lived, and a fourth by what he did. Additional names of this kind changed in every generation. The son of John White might be William Black, the son of John William's son would probably be James John's son. It was easier, however, to prove that you were the son of your father—and inherit his lands or property—if you had a second name identical with his. Sooner or later, therefore, these additional names became 'frozen' in one family after another, first among the land-owning classes and then among their tenants and servants. This additional 'frozen' name was a surname.

Surnames did not become general in Orkney until the fourteenth and fifteenth centuries.

Today an infant is still baptised with a name or names only, but the local registrar has a space in his register of births for both names and surnames and expects to get them both.

The world of law and order, school registers and telephone directories, postage and pensions, expects each and all of us to have a surname as well as a first or 'christian' name.

Christian Names

The christian name was formerly the name given to a child in baptism, but the term is now used, with the small 'c', for names given to a child whether baptised or not. The law now allows application to be made to the Registrar General for recording a change of name (or of surname) after the original name or surname has been registered at the local registration office. One kind of change that can be recorded occurs when a child's birth is registered with one name, for example, Janet, but the child is baptised in another name, for example, Barbara. Such things happen even in quite well-regulated families.

In Orkney most christian names belong to the common stock of names in use in Scotland and indeed throughout western Europe. For boys and girls there are a few common ones, for example, John, James, William, Robert, Thomas, Alexander; Margaret, Elizabeth, Mary, Anne. Then follow a number of names occurring occasionally but not so frequently; and lastly a variety of less usual names which parents choose because they are unusual, sometimes happily and sometimes without much sympathy for their defenceless infants. Fashion plays a bigger part in the choice of female names than in the choice of male ones. In 1958 the Registrar-General reported that Linda came fourth in popularity after Margaret, Elizabeth, and Mary, with 1,657 occurrences in Scotland. Of these Lindas, seven were registered in Orkney.

There are some names of Norse origin, however, which have survived in Orkney or which have been revived in families who were interested in Orkney's historic past. Here are some of these names, and the names of the men and women in *Orkneyinga Saga* who bore them:

Magnus	The greatest Magnus was St Magnus the Earl.
Harald	Earl Harald Maddadsson, d. 1206.
Rognvald	Earl Rognvald Kali, d. 1158.
Eric	Earl Rognvald married his daughter to a man called Eirik Stay-brails.
Sigurd	Earl Sigurd the Stout, who died in the Battle of Clontarf, 1014.
Olaf	Olaf, father of Sweyn of Gairsay (12th century). Olay and Olaw were common names in the 16th and 17th centuries.
Erlend	The first Earl Erlend was the son of Turf-Einar (10th century).
Ivor, Ivar	The Orkney chieftain Havard Gunnason had a grandson named Ivar (12th century).
Thora	St Magnus' mother was called Thora.
Frida	Name of the daughter of Kolbein Hruga of Wyre (12th century).
Helga	A certain Helga Moddan's daughter, born in Caithness, was at the Yule feast at Orphir in October 1128 when Earl Harald Hakonsson met his death by putting on a poisoned shirt.
Ingrid	The old Norse form was Ingirith, and three noble ladies in 12th century Orkney had this name.
Inga Brenda	There is no trace of these names in ancient Orkney, but they were in use in other Scandinavian lands.

The first Magnus seems to have been Magnus I, king of Denmark (d. 1047), who was named after the Emperor Charlemagne or 'Charles the Great', which was written by Latin chroniclers as *Carolus Magnus*.

Harald is a still older name. It came from a Primitive Norse name *Harja-valdur*, meaning 'lord-of-war'. Tacitus, the Latin historian of the first century A.D., spells this old name *Harjavalta*.

Eirik, now Eric, meant 'eternal-ruler'. Olaf meant originally something like 'son-of-his-ancestors'.

Frida meant 'fair'. Helga, 'holy'. Thora was the feminine form of the god's name Thor.

Surnames

Surnames tell a more varied story. In Orkney we find the four main groups which have already been mentioned:

   (i) those that were originally nicknames,
  (ii) patronymics, that is to say, surnames like Williamson, 'the son of William',
 (iii) territorial surnames,
 (iv) occupational surnames.

The Norsemen of old took a strong delight in using nicknames to identify particular persons. A great many of these have survived in the historical and biographical sagas written in Iceland in the twelfth and thirteenth centuries. We are unlikely to forget King Sigtrygg Silky-Beard and King Magnus Barelegs. *Orkneyinga Saga* records the names of over a score of Orkneymen with nicknames which are often picturesque and sometimes curious.

Here are some:

> Thorfinnr Hausakljúfr, 'Skull-splitter'.
> Kolbeinn Hrúga, 'Lump'.
> Hakon Kló, 'Claw'.
> Thorkell Krókauga, 'Crook-eye', 'Cross-eye'.
> Thorkell Flettir, 'Flayer'.

We still know **Kolbeinn Hrúga** as 'Cubbie Roo' who owned the castle whose ruins can still be seen in the island of Wyre. **Kló** is fossilised in the first syllable of **Clouston**. The only nickname that is very much alive today is **Flettir**. It appears again in Kolbein Flaet (1427), Mawnus Flet (1480), James Flet in Harray (1613), and so on until today. What kind of 'Flayer' was Thorkell, who was a farmer of some importance in Westray in the twelfth century? Probably not a butcher or 'flesher'. Just possibly a skinflint, or a hard landlord. Or perhaps a skilled leather-worker. The great company of the Fletts may know the secret.

Patronymics seem to have come into use in the Old Norse world quite early. Orkney people with the following surnames can be fairly sure that they have Norse ancestors:

Manson   from O.N. **Magnússon**
             (In Ireland this became MacManus)
Eunson   from O.N. **Jónsson**
Omond   from O.N. **Ámundason**
Turfus   from O.N. **Thorfinsson**
Harrold   from O.N. **Haraldsson**

There may not seem much connection between, say, **Thorfinsson** and **Turfus**. But there is a record of a man called **Torphison** in Sanday in 1601, and he provides one link. Losing the ending 'son' at some stage down the centuries was not uncommon in English surnames also; probably Tompkins was once Tompkinson.

Next we come to the territorial surnames. These came into use in western Europe among the land-owning classes, and were common in Scotland by the fourteenth century. First one finds in the records names like **David de Hamylton, John de Erskyn**, which the lawyers of the day thought to be the proper way of writing down David of Hamilton and John of Erskyn. But sooner or later the 'of' was dropped. Both methods of transcribing territorial surnames found their way to Orkney with the Scots families who obtained lands there in the late fourteenth and fifteenth centuries, when the following township names appear among the Orkney surnames:

Paplay, Holm   Linklater, Sandwick
Ireland, Stenness   Heddle, Firth
Kirkness, Sandwick Rendall

Many of these names appear first with 'of' before them: **Sigurd of Pappley** in 1369; **Wilyeam of Hedeill** in 1509. But by 1578 we find **Magnus Papla** a burgess of Kirkwall. By 1584 we have **William Heddle of that Ilk**, which meant 'of that same place'.

No doubt the owner of the township took the township name first, and then his relatives and his household, and then perhaps some of his farm servants and tenants.

Mr J. Storer Clouston, in a study of surnames written over forty years ago*—to which this chapter owes much—remarked that the greatest number of these township surnames came from the west Mainland. In Harray we find Corrigall, Brough, and Isbister. In Sandwick, as well as the Linklaters and Kirknesses, we have the Hourstons and the Garsons. From Birsay came the Marwicks, the Twatts, the Sabistons, and the Cumlaquoys. From Firth the Firths, Scarths, and Heddles. Farther afield we have the families of Halcro, Windwick, Flaws, and Berstane from South Ronaldsay; Ingsgar, now Inkster, and Corsie from Rousay; Seatter from Walls; and so on.

There are thus Orkney surnames in plenty, and an unusually high proportion of them are territorial surnames. But there are others which are often thought of as typically Orcadian, although the Orkney connection is not at first sight at all clear. Among these are names like Sinclair, Irving, Craigie, Cromarty, Leask, Moodie, Tulloch, and Louttit. These are in fact the names of Scottish families who acquired lands in Orkney by gift or purchase by the end of the sixteenth century. For example, John Cromarty bought land in Garay in South Ronaldsay in 1479. William Irving appears as the 'good-man' of Sebay in 1424. The first Louttit was Piers Loutfut of Lyking in Sandwick in the fifteenth century and he probably belonged to a branch of the Loutfuts of Strathearn in Perthshire. Later came families with Lowland Scottish surnames of all kinds, among them some with occupational names which are still common in Orkney—Smith, Shearer, Sclater, and perhaps Fiddler.

Orkney surnames thus lie in strata, each telling us something about the immigrants to the islands over the centuries and their habits of name-giving.

REFERENCE

* J. Storer Clouston, 'The People and Surnames of Orkney', in *Proceedings of the Orkney Antiquarian Society*, vol. II, 1924, pp. 31-6.

10

THE ORCADIAN IN CANADA

SOMETIME after World War I an elderly Orcadian mother who had had several letters from her son in Canada said, 'Canada's no like Orkney.' She did not have size in mind. She had heard of the summer heat with its hordes of mosquitoes and its danger of sunstroke. She had heard of the intense winter cold that yearly left some lonely person frozen in bed—one either without fuel or neglectful of keeping the fire going all night—and she had heard of young families suffocated in a burning house. On occasion her son had had to write in pencil, the ink being frozen in the bottle. Although rural life in the Canadian West is much more safe and comfortable now, Canada is still not at all like Orkney; yet along the rivers and highways the Orkney surname is common, and the Orkney place-name appears. In Manitoba there is a Binscarth and a Westray; in Saskatchewan there is a Birsay and an Orkney; and in Alberta there is a Scapa and a Kirkwall. Away up in Arctic Victoria Island there is Stromness Bay.

In the years between 1850 and 1950 Orcadians came to settle in Canada by the hundred. Other Nordic races, however, came by the thousand, as did Orientals, and the Slavs came in hundreds of thousands. Today there may be little pockets of Orcadians in Canada identifying themselves as Orcadians, but at one time the Orkney group was considerable, and a force of sufficient numbers to be spoken of as *The Orcadians*. This was so in Manitoba, in the early days of the Hudson's Bay Company.

It is definite that the company employed Orcadians for its overseas service in 1702; it may have employed them earlier. In 1702 Captain Grimmington was instructed to call at Orkney and enlist ten or twelve young men suitable for the service. Since Stromness was his last port of call before he faced the Atlantic, Grimmington must have known he could get the men at Stromness—or the company knew.

Rupert's Land

The company received its charter from Charles II in 1670. It was granted exclusive trading rights and governing rights in Rupert's Land, the land drained by rivers flowing into Hudson Bay. To this vast territory, part of Canada since 1867, came the Orkneymen enlisted at Stromness, and they were first employed at or around the forts built at the mouths of the Eastmain, the Rupert, the Moose, the Albany (all flowing into James Bay), the Severn, the Hayes (York Fort), and the Churchill.

The company wanted sober, industrious, dependable, strong, and healthy young men. The reports of the officers indicate that the Orkneymen filled the requirements; as a result Orcadians were employed in increasing numbers until the Napoleonic Wars drained the islands of young men. Soon after Waterloo the company absorbed its great rival, the North West Company, and took over many of its servants. Where two posts once traded, one was used after the union. By this time also the offspring of Orcadians and native women had grown up to learn the work of the fur trade. Henceforth fewer men were enlisted in Orkney.

Between 1700 and 1800 the number of Orcadians serving in Canada had increased from about a dozen to 416. In 1799 the company had 530 men in North America; almost four out of five were Orkneymen. It would seem that for a time an average of 70 men enlisted yearly. They contracted to serve for five years, and many remained for a second period. In 1778 the number of Orcadians engaged was smaller than usual and yet 63 were enlisted. These comprised a writer—Alexander Kennedy who rose to be chief factor—a bricklayer, a craft master, a tailor, a shipwright, a boatbuilder, a sawyer, 2 steersmen, 3 blacksmiths, 6 sailors, and 45 labourers. A number of Orcadians engaged as labourers rose in the service, because in addition to other abilities they could read and write.

Joseph Isbister

One of the first to become chief factor was the son of a Stromness merchant. Joseph Isbister appears in the company records of 1726 as a sailor. In 1740 he was appointed chief factor at Albany and is thus described in H.B. Record Society Papers:

'Joseph Isbister proved to be a man long practised in the fur trade, of great strength, independence of mind (he later denied even the London Committee's right to interfere with his command), who set to work to check the irregularities and to overcome that height of insolence that threatens to demolish all forms of government.'

Isbister enforced discipline, and pushed trade inland to check the advance of French traders from Montreal—Canada on the St Lawrence was still in French hands. Henley House, set up by Isbister 120 miles up the Albany River, was the company's first inland post. In 1748 Isbister was made commander-in-chief at Fort Prince of Wales on the Churchill. Later he returned to his command at Albany, but in 1756 the London Committee recalled him to London. He had 'checked irregularities' beyond their expectations, for he had executed three Indians for their share in a Henley House massacre. The company, however, made him a money grant. He became an independent trader working from the St Lawrence, and thus a rival of the company. In 1770 the London Committee asked him to come to London to discuss certain proposals he had made to them, evidently for the furtherance of their trade, but Isbister died in Canada in 1771.

William Tomison

By this time another Orkneyman was being noted by the company. William Tomison of South Ronaldsay joined as a labourer in 1760 and worked at York Fort. He was transferred to Severn, from which post he made two expeditions inland, going as far as Lake Manitoba, in a vain attempt to persuade the Indians to take their furs to the Bay instead of trading with the pedlars from Montreal. Canada was now in British hands. In 1776 Tomison was appointed Master at Cumberland House on the Saskatchewan. Thereafter for over twenty years he was a dominant figure, pushing the company's posts up the Saskatchewan to where Edmonton now stands, where he built a fort. Between Cumberland and Edmonton five inland posts were built either by Tomison or under his direction and were named: Upper Hudson House, Hudson's Bay House, South Branch House, Manchester House, and Buckingham House. Tomison's handling of truculent Indians and his stout resistance to the brutal pedlars marked him as a stern and dogged character. But the finest chapter in his story is his care for the Indians during the smallpox epidemic of 1781-2, and it is of special interest here, for the men who helped him with his humane work were chiefly Orcadians.

The epidemic seems to have started down on the Mississippi. The Piegans had crept up to the tents of the Snake Indians. With their knives ready for the scalping they burst into the tents, to find only the dead and the dying. They slunk away, and were later horrified to find that they had caught the disease. They could not understand this, for they reasoned that a man could no more give his sickness to another than he could give his wound. The evidence of infection so changed their views that they would not touch an afflicted man, not even to bury him. The smallpox spread rapidly to Canada and over the plains.

On 11 December 1781, Tomison records that some Indians brought him news of Indians starving, and dying of some disease. One of his visitors had violent pains in her back and was vomiting badly. Six days later Tomison had his suspicions confirmed, for his subordinate, Walker, at Hudson's House, sent down river eight men whom he could maintain no longer, food being scarce. Walker reported that the Indians were lying around the Barren Ground like rotten sheep, their tents left standing, and the wild beasts devouring them.

For months Tomison and his men did what they could for the stricken Indians. They accommodated as many as possible within their stockade, and attended these night and day. With these Indians they shared their scanty food supply, 'though God knows we can ill afford it', writes Tomison. Indians that could not be admitted camped outside. Tomison supplied them with fishing tackle and had his men cut firewood for them. The white men worked to the point of exhaustion, cutting down trees, fishing, attending the sick, bringing in the dead and the dying, making coffins and burying the dead. Much of this was done in winter. Digging a grave in ground frozen as hard as rock to a depth of several feet meant burning the ground and chopping the earth with axes. The hazard of fire within the fort from the huge fires that had to be kept burning was very great. Tomison's journal tells a pathetic tale of what he calls 'as shocking an affair as ever was known'.

Like a prairie fire the epidemic burned itself out. Many of the Indian trappers died, but, though Tomison was apprehensive over the months, not one white man was stricken. Flower of sulphur was their only protection. The Orkneymen with Tomison in his work of mercy were: Magnus Annal, James Banks, Andrew Corrigall, Robert Davy, John Drever, William Flett, William Folster, William Grey, Thomas Johnston, George Ross, Malcolm Ross, James Sandison, Magnus Sclater, James Tait, Magnus Twatt, James Wass, and Edward Wishart.

Tomison first retired in 1803 but returned to the company in 1806. He was no longer a dominant figure and seems to have done his reputation harm rather than good. In 1811, fifty-one years after he first joined the company, he retired again to Orkney, where his name is honoured as the founder of Tomison's School.

It must be understood that the Indians had to be spoken to in their own language. The company surveyor, Philip Turner, says that Tomison, Charles Isham, and Malcolm Ross were notably able to speak the Indian tongue. Isham, a half-breed, grew up with it. Malcolm Ross, from South Ronaldsay, joined the company in 1774, when he was nineteen. He is described as a young man of great veracity, an excellent canoeman, a sure shot, and much beloved by the Indians. Ross, first a labourer, was soon given a position of trust, and did much exploring, living off the land as he travelled. In 1798 he was appointed to super-intend the company's business in Athabasca, but in making a river trip alone in that region he fell from his canoe and was drowned. His early death was a severe blow to the company.

The North West Company

The pedlars from the St Lawrence banded together in the North West Company in 1779. The servants of this company, a bitter foe of the Hudson's Bay Company, often sought to overawe the Orcadians. Hudson's Bay men were at a disadvantage from the first, since their orders were not to provoke quarrels and not to retaliate—and yet not to be imposed upon. Thus the initiative lay with the North Westers, and the situation soon got out of hand. An example of what happened is given in the well-known story of John Mowat, described as a par-ticularly dour Orcadian. In 1808 at Eagle Lake a drunk North Wester, Aeneas Macdonell, armed with cutlass and pistols, was running amok among the Indians, terrifying them. He had wounded one Orcadian and was chasing another into the woods when Mowat shot him dead. The three Orcadians were seized by the North West Company, kept in irons all winter, and then sent down to Montreal where they were tried. There the North West Company controlled the courts in the fashion of the Campbells in Argyll, as described in *Kidnapped*. The three were condemned to death, but the Hudson's Bay counsel managed to have pardon offered them. Mowat refused the pardon, saying that he should never have been condemned in the first place. After being branded with an iron as felons the three served a six months' sentence.

Union of the Trading Companies

The coming of the Selkirk settlers in 1811, among the first of whom were several Orcadians, brought the quarrel of the two companies to a head. The massacre at Seven Oaks in 1816 of Governor Semple and his twenty-odd followers, most of them unarmed or badly armed Orkneymen, led to government inquiry, and, in a few years, to union. This union of the two companies in 1821 and the beginning of settle-ment marked the end of an era. Fewer men were enlisted in Orkney, and Orkneymen retiring from the service often chose to take the company's land grant at Red River in lieu of a passage home, especially those with native wives. A number of the offspring of Orcadians and Indians distinguished themselves in early Manitoba, such as John Norquay, premier of Manitoba, and Alexander Kennedy Isbister, grandson of the writer who enlisted in 1778, the scholar and benefactor of Manitoba University. For a time the Orkney element was numerous on the Red River, but the great influx of settlers in the late nineteenth century swamped them. The children of men who had been coming and going for two hundred years saw the influx, and heard the title of pioneers being given to the incomers.

Orcadians were still enlisted at Stromness after the union of 1821, but the practice stopped when the company's ships ceased to call there in 1891. The Shetland writer, Isaac Cowie, in *The Company of Adventurers*, and the Stromness writer, N. M. W. J. McKenzie, in *The Men of the Hudson's Bay Company*, both tell of Orcadians they met in their travels in the late nineteenth and the early twentieth centuries. Before their day a man born, raised, and buried in Orkney made his name known as one of the foremost Arctic explorers. As he was an officer in the company his story is written in Volume XVI, Hudson's Bay Record Society Papers, *Rae's Arctic Correspondence*.

John Rae

According to a letter he wrote to a friend after his wanderings were over, John Rae travelled 2,910 miles inland and 3,645 miles on or near the Arctic Coast on foot, and on the Arctic in boats he voyaged 6,700 miles. He surveyed 1,765 miles of new land and coastline, of which 1,135 were added to the charts. He contributed thirty scientific papers to the Royal Geographic Society or other institutions. He made five trips into the Arctic, two from Hudson's Bay for exploration purposes, and three from the Great Bear area to search for the missing Franklin and his ships. Ironically he discovered the fate of Franklin and purchased items belonging to that gallant captain and to his officers from Eskimoes while he was on an exploration trip.

The story of all this is so vast that it cannot be told here. His first trip to the Arctic, undertaken to complete the survey of the northern continental coast, is interesting because he had with him ten men of whom four were from Orkney. They were George Flett from Birsay and John Corrigal from Orphir, both steersmen, and, as middlemen, John Folster of Firth, Edward Hutchison of Papa Westray, a Shetlander, a Hebridean, two French-Canadians, a boy from York Fort, and an Indian deer hunter. Rae gave his men great praise for their spirit and endurance, singling out Flett, Corrigal, and Folster for special praise. For a later expedition Rae asked Sir George Simpson to get Corrigal and Folster for him—Flett was dead by this time—but for some reason the two were not contacted.

It is to be noted that Rae's travels were much different from the famous journeys of Mackenzie and Fraser. Rae and his men lived off the land, and travelled on sea and land; the other two travelled in a well-provisioned canoe with a disciplined crew, going only where the river went and sure of finding their way back. They had their river dangers, of course; yet Rae in later life navigated hundreds of miles on the dangerous Fraser alone in a dug-out canoe.

Rae's memorial in St Magnus Cathedral deeply impressed Wilson of the Antarctic. He wrote of it, quoting the epitaph:

'John Rae, M.D., LL.D., F.R.S., F.R.G.S., Arctic Explorer, Intrepid Discoverer of the fate of Sir John Franklin's last Expedition. Born 1813. Died 1893. Expeditions 1846–47, 1848–49, 1851–52, 1853–54.' This is the whole inscription—and the man is a life-sized figure lying asleep wrapped in a sleeping bag with moccasins on and a gun, and book open by his side.

Rae's story has enriched the history of Orkney; it is fitting that his dust added richness to that already rich dust round St Magnus Cathedral.

From the western Arctic to Red River, and from Red River to Ungava, Orcadians of the eighteenth and nineteenth centuries made paths, hewed clearings, built portages, erected buildings, and planted gardens in the wilderness that was Rupert's Land. These have become the roads and the river landings, the airfields and the towns, and the cultivated fields of the Canada we know today.

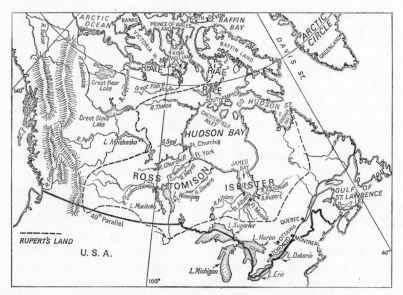

FIG. 3 This map shows the territory in which the fur traders worked.

ST MAGNUS CATHEDRAL

Earl Rognvald's Vow

ELSEWHERE in this book the tale has been told of the noble life and Christian martyrdom of Earl Magnus the Holy, for a Christian martyrdom undoubtedly it was. His cousin and murderer, Earl Hakon, was equally a professed Christian, but it is clear that he—and even more those fiercer men behind him who impelled him to the deed—stood for the old wild Viking ways, rooted as they were in an immemorial pagan past. Earl Magnus, however, personified the gentler spirit and merciful ideals that were associated with the new faith.

Also in this book is told the tale of how the martyred earl's nephew, Rognvald, set out to recover his share of his patrimony; and how, after a first unsuccessful attempt, he swore that, should he succeed in a second venture, he would build at Kirkwall a stone minster 'more magnificent than any other in these lands', and that the relics of the holy martyr should be brought from his grave at Birsay and buried in the new cathedral that ever more would bear his name. And right nobly did the good Earl Rognvald fulfil his pious vow—though only a portion of the stately building that we so admire today was erected during his lifetime, and the completion of the cathedral was not achieved until more than three centuries had passed.

Work started in 1137. The business management of the great enterprise was in the capable hands of the earl's father, Kol, who raised the ready cash by an ingenious arrangement with the udallers or landholders, whom he permitted to free themselves from all further taxation in respect of their estates by a lump sum paid down. Earl Rognvald himself was a man of taste and culture. Both he and the bishop, William the Old, described as 'a good Parisian scholar', no doubt had much to say as to the design and decoration of their new minster. But the actual deviser of the building—the architect as we should nowadays call him, though in the Middle Ages he was termed the master-mason—is unknown. It is, however, extremely probable that both the master-mason and the 'free-masons'—those who were responsible for the dressed stone work, as distinct from the 'rough-masons' who built the rubble walls—came from Durham, the grandest of British Norman cathedrals.

The Norman Style of Architecture

In 1152 Earl Rognvald and Bishop William went off on a pilgrimage to the Holy Land. Their journey there and back is told at length, with much picturesque detail, in the *Orkneyinga Saga*. It is most unlikely that they would set off had not at least the choir, containing the high altar, been completed, so that the church might be consecrated before they left upon a long and hazardous expedition from which they might never return. The cathedral was designed in what is usually termed in Britain the Norman style of architecture, since its full development in this country came after the Norman Conquest. More properly, speaking for western Europe as a whole, we may describe this style as Romanesque, since it is really the old Roman manner of building, modified but never wholly forgotten during the early Middle Ages. Its distinguishing marks are bulky cylindrical piers, heavy round arches, and certain characteristic forms of decoration, of which one of the most favoured is the chevron.

A cathedral is so styled because it is the head church of a diocese, and therefore contains the bishop's throne (*cathedra*). Such a church, being large and important, was usually designed in the form of a cross. The short eastern end, or head of the cross, formed the choir or chancel, where stood the high altar. The long western limb, or shaft of the cross, is the nave, and was set aside for the general congregation. The two lateral arms of the cross, known as the transepts, usually contained small chapels or altars dedicated to various saints. In the centre rose a tower, and the space underneath, termed the crossing, together with the western portion of the chancel, contained the stalls of the clergy and choristers.

The Plan

As we see it today, it is obvious from the first glance at its exterior that Kirkwall Cathedral conforms to the standard cruciform plan. Nevertheless, it has been greatly altered from the original plan proposed by Earl Rognvald and Bishop William. What they set out to build was a church comprising (1) a short choir of three bays, terminating in a semi-circular apse designed to house the high altar; (2) short transepts, each with an 'apsidiole' or miniature apse projecting from the east side; and (3) a nave of eight bays, probably intended to have two western towers, as at Durham. Over the crossing also was planned a low central tower. Both nave and choir had vaulted aisles, but the other parts of the church were ceiled with wood.

Of this original building programme there remain today the three bays of the choir, extending eastward from the crossing, with their vaulted side-aisles; approximately three bays of the nave and its aisles; and the two transepts, each of which has a spiral staircase in a specially large buttress respectively at the north-east and south-west corner. Externally, this early work is built of well-coursed grey flagstone rubble, probably from the Ayre, with red or yellow sandstone corners. The red sandstone seems to have been brought from the Head of Holland, the yellow or white sandstone probably from Eday. Internally the walls are built partly of rubble and partly of dressed sandstone; and in the south transept the eastern wall is built in alternate courses of red and yellow stone. This is the earliest example in our cathedral of the use of 'polychrome' work, which becomes such a striking feature in the three great western portals. The massive cylindrical piers are built of dressed sandstone, and the capitals, from which the round arches spring, are enriched in the usual Norman fashion.

The Nave

While all the piers of the nave and the round arches connecting them, as well as the round arches of the 'triforium'—as the open area or passage above the main arcade is called—are more or less similar, there are differences between them, for example in the mouldings of the capitals and bases. Some of the piers show in their lower portions signs of weathering, as if they had stood in the open air for a considerable period. The upper portions of such piers look fresher and newer, and in some the tint of the stone is different. From all this it is clear that the building of the nave, as the masons worked from the crossing westwards, must have lasted a considerable time; extending (so it would seem) into the early years of the thirteenth century. In fact, we know that for a long time the western end of the uncompleted nave was shut off by a temporary gable wall, between the sixth pair of piers counting westward from the crossing. The foundation of this wall was laid bare during the restoration of the cathedral in the early years of this century.

Above the triforium is the 'clearstorey', a row of high windows lighting the ceiling. These windows are pointed; they belong to the Gothic style of architecture, which superseded the Norman style towards the end of the twelfth century. The vaulted ceiling of the nave was not completed until well on in this century: the two westmost bays were never vaulted at all, but were covered by a wooden roof, until during the restoration they were vaulted to conform with the rest. The nave vault, unlike that in the choir, has no ridge-rib, which gives it a weak effect. It is badly cracked; and the westmost pier on the north

St Magnus Cathedral, from the south-east

St Magnus Cathedral—the Rae Memorial

St Magnus Cathedral—the nave

side is tilted towards the west. Obviously there is a weakness in the foundation here; and this defect may have been the reason why the original design (if in fact it was the original design) for two western towers was discarded. The nave aisles are vaulted, also without a ridge-rib. Polychrome work is visible in the south-western 'respond' or half-pier which terminates the arcade, and also on the insides of the three western portals.

The Crossing

The four great piers of the crossing carry the weight of the central tower. These magnificent clustered pillars and the four soaring pointed arches which spring from them are not built in the old Norman or Romanesque style. Their rich mouldings and the foliage carved on their capitals are typical of what is called the 'Transitional' period between the Norman and the 'First Pointed' style which is the earliest phase of true Gothic. It is therefore evident that these four pillars, as we now have them, must date from about the year 1200. Of course they must have had Norman predecessors, and it remains somewhat of a mystery why the latter should have been replaced after so short a period had elapsed. We can hardly believe that a Norman central tower had collapsed, for such a catastrophe would have wrecked the adjoining parts of the church, east and west and north and south—where the earliest work, dating from Earl Rognvald's first building programme, survives intact. It may be that about 1200 the builders decided to have a lofty tower, and that the original Norman pillars were deemed inadequate to support its weight. Or it may be simply that they desired to have the four great central pillars of the church built in the latest fashion. It is worth noting that at Jedburgh Abbey, and at the 'town's kirk' of St Nicholas in Aberdeen, the four piers of the crossing are of Transitional date, though all around them is Norman masonry.

The Choir

The three western bays of the choir are in the Norman style, using polychrome masonry in the triforium arches, the arch stones being alternately of red and yellow sandstone. The east end, from the third bay beyond the crossing, is in a totally different style; and the change in the masonry is clearly seen in the whole height of the walls on either side. What happened was that about the year 1220 the old Norman semi-circular apse was taken down and the choir enlarged by building on three more bays, with a square eastern end. This new work is in the richest and loveliest First Pointed Gothic, virginal in its purity and grace. On the capitals of the clustered piers are richly carved foliage

6

and figure sculpture. It seems likely that these capitals were carved by craftsmen imported from France, or at least by men who had been trained in that country. Nevertheless, the choir as a whole was clearly designed by an English master-mason, as appears by its square eastern end; for in the French cathedrals the east end has usually a multangular termination.

When the cathedral was restored, the foundation of the semi-circular Norman apse was found under the floor of the extended choir.

The Transepts

The transepts have wooden roofs and in both the side walls have been heightened. In their lower parts the west walls and gables of both transepts are decorated with a very beautiful intersecting arcade of Norman workmanship; but in the gable of the south transept this arcade has been interrupted by the insertion of a thirteenth-century door, the pointed arch of which is built in polychrome work. Like the nave and chancel the transepts are fully designed with a triforium and a clearstorey. In the east wall of each transept an arched opening led into the original Norman apsidioles; but in the thirteenth century these were replaced by small square vaulted chapels, now used as vestries respectively for the minister and the choir.

The Interior: General

The first impression formed from inspecting the interior of the cathedral is the feeling of great size. Yet Kirkwall Cathedral is really quite small, compared with the English and French cathedral churches, or even compared with St Andrews Cathedral and Glasgow Cathedral in our own country. The illusion of size is due to the perfect proportion of the interiors, and in particular to the remarkable narrowness of the nave, which creates an immediate effect of loftiness. The second impression which remains in one's mind is that of the beautiful mellow colouring of the stone work—the grey flags, the warm reds and yellows of the sandstone. Yet this is, comparatively speaking, a charm of modern date; since in the Middle Ages the entire inner surfaces of the church, walls and pillars alike, were richly painted, glowing with portrayals of angels and saints, or enriched with decorative patterns in varied hues. Traces of this ancient colouring may still be detected in different parts of the church.

Nobody in the Middle Ages ever obtained a vista of a great church from end to end. Between the two western piers of the crossing stretched the rood-loft, a carved oaken screen separating the nave from the choir, and carrying on its upper platform a great rood, that is to say, a painted wooden figure-group of the Crucified Saviour with St Mary and St John on either hand. In somewhat the same way, the view is interrupted today by the finely carved choir stalls, which, with the pulpit, all date from the modern restoration. Previous to that time only the choir was in use as the parish church, and was shut off from the rest of the cathedral by a paltry glass screen.

Exterior : The Western Portals

The glory of Kirkwall Cathedral, seen from the outside, is the three great western portals—a large central one admitting to the nave, with smaller doors on either side by which the aisles may be entered. All three are in the full Gothic style of the early thirteenth century: all have pointed arches variously moulded, and richly carved bases and capitals, though the finely wrought detail has suffered sorely from centuries of exposure to the weather. The successive 'orders', or rings of mouldings round the arches, are carried by a series of shafts, each made of a single long stone; but all these have been replaced in modern times. In the great central door these shafts are 'staggered', that is to say, they are set alternately in a forward and retired position. The superior dignity of the central doorway is emphasised not only by its greater size—and by the fact that it is built in five orders, whereas the lateral doorways have only four—but also because it is set in a shallow projecting porch, terminating above in a gable. In the apex of this gable is a shield with a bishop's crozier. The shield displays the arms of the Hay family; but no bishop bearing this name is known to have occupied the see of Orkney.

The most exciting thing about these western portals is the varied use of polychrome work. In the great central arch the method selected was to make each ring or order of the arch alternately of red and white sandstone—and, in all probability, the original shafts which supported these orders were similarly made of alternate coloured stones. The north aisle portal is treated in the same way; but in the south aisle portal the method used is to make each separate arch stone, which traverses the whole series of orders from inside to outside of the arch, alternately of white and red stone. The lower parts of the buttress between the central portal and the north aisle, and of the exterior corner buttress of this aisle are built in polychrome work. The effect produced by the use of varied colouring in the stones gives the west front of our cathedral a magnificent effect.

The upper part of the west front was completed at a later date, probably in the fifteenth century. It is in a greatly inferior style to the noble conception embodied in the three great portals. To begin with, the west window does not spread across the entire space between the two lateral buttresses of the nave. It has, therefore, a somewhat inadequate appearance. In itself the window is an attractive piece of design. It contains five pointed lights, with plain intersecting or 'basket' tracery in the pointed general arch, and a 'transom' or cross-bar, which is triplicated in each of the window lights.

The North Front of the Nave

The first two bays of the aisle are made of deep-red sandstone ashlar —i.e. squared blocks—and among the stones are many portions of half-round pillars, which must have been prepared for the completion of the nave before the work was interrupted, and in the end were used to make up the later walling. The buttresses in this comparatively late portion of the aisle are much bolder in projection than that of the Norman work farther east; also the lancet windows here have trefoiled heads—another sign of late work. These are the only trefoiled windows in the cathedral.

In the bay next eastward is the loveliest door in the whole cathedral. Dating from about 1200 it is round-arched and richly moulded, with stiff-leaf foliage and three shafts corresponding to the orders of the arch. This beautiful doorway has been much restored, but in strict correspondence with the original design. The whole of the bay is built of red sandstone ashlar.

The next two bays of the north aisle are late twelfth-century work, joining on to the three eastmost bays, which are part of Earl Rognvald's original cathedral. All this work is built in grey flagstone rubble masonry, with red sandstone dressings.

Above the whole length of the aisle are the windows of the clear-storey. These are work of the thirteenth century, except for the westmost, which belong to the fifteenth-century completion of the nave. Except for these two bays the clearstorey is all built in white sandstone.

The North Transept

The lower part of the north transept is again Norman work of the original building effort. The extra large buttress at the western corner contains a stair by which one reached the triforium galleries and the central tower. Above the Norman work, as usual built of flagstone rubble, comes later work in red sandstone, and over all, on the front of the transept, a great circular window. On the east side of the transept the square eastern chapel, which in the thirteenth century replaced the original Norman apsidiole, once stood free from the choir, but has later been united with the latter.

The Choir and East Front

In the choir the first two bays beyond the side chapel are Earl Rognvald's work, in flagstone rubble, while the rest is of the early thirteenth century, with Gothic windows, but built all in flagstone rubble—as if for some reason the supply of sandstone at that time was running short. Nevertheless the clearstorey was in due course built in red ashlar; moreover, at some period later in the thirteenth century, the wall was heightened, but in white ashlar. When the wall was raised, thirty-six grotesquely carved corbels which had supported the original Norman parapet were carefully built into the new masonry—obviously because the later builders liked them and thought them worth preserving.

Except for modern restoration, the great east front of the cathedral is all work of the thirteenth century. It is a far finer composition than the west facade. This is due mainly to the noble proportions of the great east window, which with its four lights and splendid rose completely fills up the space between the two flanking buttresses.

The South Front and the Central Tower

In a general way the south side of the choir reproduces the architectural features of the opposite side, the first three bays from the east end being the thirteenth-century extension, while the remaining two, up to the transeptal side-chapel, are Earl Rognvald's work. In the clearstorey of this portion there are five Norman corbels of the original parapet—before the wall was heightened. The higher level is built in red ashlar. In the first bay of the extended work is a fine priests' door, dating from about 1250. On this side also the gap between the transeptal chapel and the choir has later been filled in. The south transept gable is in Norman rubble, except for the two uppermost stages, which are mostly modern. The doorway here (already noted as an insertion of the thirteenth century) shows yet another ingenious method of using polychrome work: the pointed arch has four orders, each built in separate arch stones of alternating colours; a red stone overlies a yellow one, and in the next course vice versa, so as to produce a curious chequer pattern.

The south side of the nave reproduces generally the same building sequence and styles of masonry as the northern side, but with certain important differences. Next to the transept are traces of a built-up Norman doorway. Five bays farther west is another doorway, which as we now have it was remodelled by Bishop Reid early in the sixteenth century. These two doors tell us that a cloister was intended here:

the foundations of its enclosing wall were discovered during the restoration.

Another point to be noted about the south side of the nave is that all the flat Norman buttresses have been reinforced. Clearly the builders were worried about their foundations on this side.

Lastly, the central tower is all built in fine red sandstone ashlar, and dates from the fourteenth century. Doubtless originally it will have had a tall spire; but this, having been destroyed by lightning in 1671, was replaced by a low pyramidal helmet, which, rebuilt in the same form in 1848, was replaced by the present copper-sheathed octagonal spire in the last restoration.

In a single brief chapter for a book such as this, there has been no space to deal with many beautiful and fascinating features about St Magnus Cathedral. If you wish further information, you will obtain it in the full and admirable account published by the Royal Commission on Ancient Monuments in their volume on the Orkneys. In particular, you will find there details of the many interesting monuments which the cathedral contains, as well as of the ancient bells, whose mellow chimes are so pleasantly familiar to the good folk of Kirkwall.

GLOSSARY

Aisle: division of church, parallel to and divided by pillars from the nave, choir or transept.
Apse: semi-circular recess, arched or dome-roofed.
Arcade: series of arches on same plane.
Buttress: support built against wall.
Capital: head or cornice of pillar.
Chevron: bent bar of V shape.
Clearstorey: part of wall of cathedral with series of windows, above aisle roofs.
Corbel: projection of stone designed to carry over sailing masonry.
Lancet: arch or window with pointed head.
Piers: pillars.
Portal: door.
Shaft: column.
Stiff-leaf: conventionally carved foliage.
Trefoiled: arranged in three lobes.

12

PLACE AND PEOPLE

THE world position of Orkney is of primary importance. Its high latitude gives long summer days, long winter nights, cool temperatures; its oceanic position brings cloud, humidity, and wind and restrains the temperature range; its spatial relationship to the rest of Europe explains the broad lines of much of its history and therefore of its peopling.

The shores of north-west Europe form a vast bay across which lie the British Isles, blocking free access to the open Atlantic. The seafaring men of these countries—and they include the greatest seafarers in the world—thus have to sail round either the south end of Britain or the north whenever they want to enter the world oceans. The southern route is the more convenient, and so the English Channel is the busiest strip of sea in the world, but some traffic goes by the north and thus the harbours of Orkney are rarely without visitors, and in times of war, when the English Channel is dangerous or even blocked, Orkney harbours are thronged. The Napoleonic Wars and both World Wars turned Orkney into a naval base, with profound results not only through ready markets for farm produce but in the stimulus provided by unkan folk[1] and their ways of life.

Natural Endowments

If Fate has been fairly kind to Orkney in history, Nature has been no less generous in her endowment of the land of Orkney. Only a small area in the north of Graemsay and west of Stromness harbour is of Highland rock: the rest is built of sedimentary rocks, sandstones, and flagstones of Old Red Sandstone date. The upper beds are gritty sandstones which—though yielding colourful building stone, as can be seen in splendour in Kirkwall Cathedral—give rise to poor acid soils. Thus Eday and Hoy, where these sandstones dominate, are agriculturally the poorest isles in Orkney and are for the most part clad in sombre heather moors. The lower beds, of which most of Orkney is built, are flagstones in great variety. Most are fine-grained and weather to a clay; others are more sandy. Some contain a high proportion of lime and some are even bituminous. All of these can be seen in the flagstone

[1] Unkan folk—strangers.

cliffs, for the different beds have differing degrees of durability and therefore weather out to different extents, forming the characteristic little ledges on the cliffs which are so convenient for nesting sea-birds. Above all, the varied flagstones yield on weathering a good mixture of fine and coarse material, just what is required to give a soil of reasonable texture. The lime content, also, tends to restrain the development of acidity which the cool moist climate encourages. Yet another valuable property of the flagstones is that they readily provide good building stone. Almost everywhere in Orkney it is easy to find a quarry which yields fairly regular blocks of stone, with two faces flat and parallel because they represent the bedding planes. Thus good building has always been cheap and easy, and no doubt this is one reason why Orkney has so many well-preserved monuments from prehistoric time and why every Orkney farmer was and still often is his own mason. When fresh, the stone is grey, but it soon weathers to a warm brown or even ochre colour and the sharp edges become rounded.

This relatively fast weathering accounts for the soft outline of the Orkney hills. Except where the tabular beds are very resistant as in Hoy and Eday, or where there is a marked alternation of stronger and weaker beds, as for example in Rousay, outcropping rock is rare and hill-slopes are usually very smooth and rarely steep. There are, moreover, extensive areas of smooth ground of very low slope, for example around the lochs of Harray and Stenness, in Tankerness, and on Shapinsay and Stronsay. A large proportion of Orkney, in fact, lies at a most convenient slope—steep enough to give some natural drainage but not too steep for ploughing. The very flat areas, which under original conditions would be peat-covered, are rarely so far from the sea as to make drainage impossible, though much of this kind of land has had to wait for modern techniques before the digging of drainage channels or laying of drains became economic. Seldom are the hill-slopes too steep to have a soil cover and thus to carry pasture or be capable of being improved from heather moorland to pasture.

The Shoreline

If we look at the underwater contours round Orkney we find that the bottom slopes gently to about twenty fathoms and then drops steeply to the Continental Shelf, which here is about forty fathoms. The slopes in the zone between present sea-level and twenty fathoms, too, are a continuation of the above-water slopes. Orkney, in fact, is a plateau whose upper surface, if reconstructed, would slope from south-west to north-east. This plateau surface however has been carved up by millions of years of erosion into a gently rolling surface, and what we see now as the sixty or so Orkney isles are simply the remnants after this rolling surface has been drowned by a submergence of the original plateau by some 120 feet. It is this drowning that gives us not only our many islands but also their intricate shoreline. This shoreline could be classified into three types.

First are the 'neutral' shores, where the land slopes smoothly down to a gently sloping rocky beach, as for example in Kirkwall Bay or St Margaret's Hope.

Second are the parts of the coast which are exposed to the full force of ocean waves which are actively eroding the land. These coasts are marked by cliffs, which naturally are most impressive where the coast is highest and the ocean stormiest. Thus all the western shores, from Tor Ness in Hoy to the Mull Head of Papa Westray, are cliffed and in places, especially Hoy, quite spectacularly so. No doubt this coast was originally gently sloping and lay farther to the west than it does now, but since the sea has been cutting into the land far faster than the land has been weathering away, the coastline has receded and the cliffs have grown higher. This can be well seen all along the west coast of the Mainland, where the gentle westward slope of the hills is sharply cut by perpendicular and often overhanging cliffs. The nature of the flags, of course, encourages the formation of cliffs: perpendicular where the bedding is horizontal; overhanging where the dip of the beds is to the sea, and sloping back where the dip is to the land.

The third type of coast is that where the sea is piling up debris, be it sand, gravel, or larger rocks. This occurs where the underwater slope is very gentle, so that the force of the breaking wave is spent in driving material up the beach, and the backwash is relatively feeble. Much also depends on what material is available on the sea bottom. Sometimes sand is thrown up in great quantities over a wide area, as in Sanday, where it gives its name to the island. An accurate map was made of Sanday in 1750 and it shows a smaller island than at present and indeed suggests that the present Sanday is formed by sand joining up a series of smaller islands.

Sometimes the gently sloping area is quite small: the Bay of Skaill is a good example of this. There must originally have been a deeply indented but shallow bay here, reaching back to Aith. The breaking waves would form a sand-bar across the bay, so shutting off the head of the bay to form the Loch of Skaill, and thereafter sand would blow steadily eastwards from the dunes at the beach, slowly filling in the loch from the west and even blowing up the slope of the hill of Kierfiold to the summit. The sand here and on many other such beaches is made almost entirely from broken shells and is thus a form of lime. The sweetening effect of this on peat moor is very striking and must have attracted the earliest settlers, for many of the oldest farm-names and parish churches are in areas of blown sand.

Where pebbles rather than sand are involved, the wave-built bars and beaches are much more restricted. Echna Loch in Burray, for example, is dammed up behind a bay-head bar of gravel. Sometimes the ebb and flow of the tides prevents the bar from forming completely and a channel remains at one side, forming an oyce or ouse, as at Finstown or Tankerness or Waulkmill Bay.

Effect of the Ice Age

But the physical build of Orkney cannot be explained without reference to yet another factor. In the comparatively recent geological past the climate of the northern hemisphere deteriorated a little, sufficient to cause the accumulation over north-west Europe of an enormous ice-sheet, which moved slowly outwards towards the open Atlantic. Orkney lay in the path of this and must have suffered much grinding and erosion of its surface by the passage of the ice. But the ice-sheet brought with it debris from the floor of the North Sea and the neighbouring lands and some of this it plastered over Orkney, and when the ice-sheet finally melted the contained rock-waste was also dumped, sometimes rather irregularly. Because the material had been brought so far, it was mostly finely broken up, a large part of it forming clay. This 'boulder clay' is found over most of Orkney, though naturally it is deeper on low, flat ground and thinner on the hill-tops and slopes. Hollows in it form lochs and occasionally its irregular hummocks are difficult to drain, as for example in the north part of Stenness, but by and large the boulder clay, especially where it was derived from sea-bottom deposits, makes good soil, sometimes better than that formed directly from the decay of bed-rock.

In the last phase of the glaciation the climate was not much worse than, say, north Finland today. The main ice-sheet had gone, but small glaciers persisted in the hills and there was intense frost-shattering of exposed rock. This must have helped considerably in smoothing off the profiles of the hills, and the traces of such frost action can often be seen in the upper foot or so of the boulder clay.

Hoy was just high enough to allow snow to accumulate on the down-wind sunless side of the highest hills, and to consolidate and move seawards as valley glaciers. Such glaciers erode in their upper parts and dump the debris where they melt. Evidence for such a glacier can be recognised just east of Hellia, at the Kame of Hoy. The huge amphi-theatre there is almost ringed by cliffs: it is, indeed, a corrie, and just above the shore and cut through by the burn is the moraine, a steep pile of angular loose rocks. There is another morainic hillock on the shore at Rackwick.

These glaciers disappeared only some ten thousand years ago, and with the amelioration of climate Neolithic man colonised Scotland. Because of the drowning of Orkney and its separation from the mainland, not all the plants and animals were as successful as man in getting into Orkney, so that while our prehistoric human remains are abundant the flora and fauna include fewer items than in Scotland.

The Influence of Climate

So far, we have considered only the characteristics of what is under our feet in Orkney: clearly what is over our heads is at least as significant to us and to the crops and animals on which we so largely depend for our livelihood.

We have already pointed out that Orkney is very much under the influence of the sea. The main air circulation is from the west, but often the indraught to a depression brings wind from the south-east as well. The temperature map of Europe shows that Orkney has the same mid-winter temperature as the south coast of England, and even Istanbul, at latitude 41°. Honesty compels us to admit, however, that in summer our temperatures are the same as those of the White Sea, which is on the Arctic Circle. We belong to a culture which talks of winter, spring, summer, and autumn, but in fact none of these seasons is clear-cut in Orkney. We can have primroses in bloom in December and January, yet harvesting can be done in oilskins and sou'-westers. Marvellous July weather with endless sun and oppressive warmth can alternate with gales that have in the past cost hundreds of fishermen's lives, and in modern times can stop even a 750-ton mailboat from crossing the Pentland Firth. Oceanic influence brings cloud and reduces the hours of sunshine: as far as prevailing winds are concerned, Orkney lies somewhat in the lee of the mainland of Scotland and so has less rain and humidity than the Outer Hebrides. On the other hand, whereas the Hebrides suffer only gales from the west, Orkney has to endure them from the east as well. This may be tiresome to people, but it means Orkney has less rainfall—some 37 inches annually—and the brisk winds dry some of this up, so that Orkney does not suffer from the excessive humidity, above and underfoot, which creates blanket bog in the Hebrides.

These conditions do not favour corn-growing, but in our time grain for bread comes from the great wheatlands of the world—from Canada, South America, and Australia—and Orcadians no longer depend on brose or bannocks of bere and oats for their daily bread. All of them eat wheaten flour, though their elders have the grace to call it 'baker's' bread to distinguish it from the indigenous grains. Orkney is able to exploit her great natural advantage. Climate and soil favour grass and thus the production of beef and milk products, both fetching high prices in the affluent modern world.

Fall in Population

Standards of living, however, have been rising in Orkney as elsewhere —and the war showed Orcadians what standards were elsewhere. One result has been redoubled application of scientific methods of agriculture and the other an amalgamation of holdings, particularly of small ones. Inevitably the population directly dependent on the land has diminished and Orkney shows a decrease of total population with every census, being only 18,650 in 1961, the lowest since the beginning of the nineteenth century when a census was first taken. In one sense it is sad that there should now be only 18,650 Orcadians compared with 32,225 at the maximum of 1861, but this decrease has been brought about not by abandonment following failure but by self-promotion to larger farms and bigger targets in Aberdeen, the Lothians, and even the English plain.

Kirkwall

The 18,650 Orcadians in 1961 are by no means evenly spread over the county. Kirkwall, the capital, had no less than 4,293 of them, and has shown a steady growth in the last half-century. This is not surprising. From Norse times its situation at the 'waist' of the Mainland, half-way between east and west Mainland, and with harbours convenient for both North and South Isles has made it the natural route focus of the isles. In the days when each parish and farm was virtually self-sufficient, Kirkwall's functions were those of an administrative, ecclesiastical, and judicial centre only, and its population was less than half of its present total. The tonnage of shipping in 1790 was 2,000 tons—equivalent to a couple of visits of a steamer of the 1960s. The modern growth—and it is so modern that Kirkwall is a 'boom town' in a modest way—is coupled to the development of specialised, scientific agriculture in the county. Orkney now exports large quantities of cattle, sheep, eggs, and cheese, and imports fertilisers, machines, fuel, building material, and other farm equipment and 'consumer durables'. Most of this trade is handled by Kirkwall, as is the servicing of machinery and vehicles; and a considerable clerical staff is necessary to deal with a complicated modern economy overlaid by a suite of government departments interesting themselves in agriculture.

The town grew up on the natural harbours of Kirkwall Bay and the Peerie Sea, and in the shadow of the cathedral, built more than eight centuries ago by the sainted Viking Rognvald in memory of his sainted and martyr forebear Magnus. (It would be interesting to know if any other county has had two of its earls canonised.) The main axis was one single street straggling past the cathedral to the harbour, lined by houses which were usually gable-on to the street and with their garden rigs stretching back from the street after the manner of many a Scottish burgh. Subsequent development filled many of these rigs with new buildings, and the town in the last forty years has sprawled over the surrounding low ground and crept quite high up the slopes on the east side. The population of Kirkwall is now stationary at about 4,300.

The cathedral, earl's and bishop's palaces lend dignity to the old town, and the original streets are picturesque but, like other towns which have grown considerably but maintained their early street system in the centre, Kirkwall has a serious traffic problem.

Stromness

The other burgh, Stromness, has a quite different background. Its fine sheltered bay and anchorage was only of local value until the Napoleonic Wars, the opening up of Canada, and the North Atlantic whale and seal fisheries brought sailing vessels in numbers to the north. Above all, the herring fishing fleet stimulated the growth of Stromness and sometimes inflated its census returns, so that early last century it recorded a larger population than Kirkwall. Both, however, were only in the two thousand range.

Two World Wars brought increased business to Stromness and its harbour, but nevertheless its population has slowly and steadily declined in the last hundred years and in 1961 it was only 1414. Modern road transport and the general tendency to centralisation has caused Orkney's urban growth to be concentrated in Kirkwall. Important as Stromness harbour is, it would require some revival of its use as a fishing base to bring about further growth. The local fishermen's co-operative is a step in this direction.

The Landward Area

Finstown owes its existence to its position at a road junction in the centre of the Mainland and to the services—mill, school, shops—which have been provided there. St Margarets Hope, once a fishing station and steamer harbour, has now reverted to the status of a local centre. Whitehall, Pierowall, and Longhope are little more than harbour hamlets since herring-fishing activities have vanished and no other influences exist to concentrate settlement in one place. Dounby, on the other hand, as a service centre in a good agricultural area, has grown somewhat in recent years.

In the rural parishes population is by no means evenly distributed. In the Orkney type of climate conditions deteriorate rapidly with increase in altitude, and thus farm-land and farm-houses are restricted to the lower ground unless some special shelter exists. This factor operates so strongly that scarcely any population is to be found above the 300-foot contour. Only on the lower islands, for example Sanday, Stronsay, and Shapinsay are the farms spread evenly, with roads covering the area. In Westray the higher west side is empty of people; in Rousay the population and roads are peripheral, and in the Mainland, areas of populated low ground are separated by hills. Indeed, in Orkney, 'hill' is synonymous with uncultivated land.

By and large, farm-houses and steadings are distributed evenly over the cultivated land, taking advantage of shelter and access to roads wherever possible. Farms are normally of compact shape with well-laid-out fields, for most of them were rationally planned within the last century and a half. Rarely do farm or field shapes have to take account of natural features as they do in so many Highland areas.

The older houses show close links with the 'long' houses of the Norse fringe of Scotland. Scarcity of timber restricted the width of the house and the stormy climate kept the height down to a single storey. Enlargement of houses could only be by extension in length, therefore, or by the duplication of buildings. Many of the older places thus consist of a single long building; house, barn, byre and other premises being on one continuous axis. Sometimes the kailyard lay opposite the house, sometimes there was another range of buildings, with for convenience a narrow 'street' or 'close' between. Flagstones not only provided good, if heavy, roofing, but tidy floors and pavements round the houses. A conspicuous feature of the old steadings, often still to be seen, was the kiln, a tower-like structure in which damp sheaves were dried to facilitate threshing, where moisture was expelled from corn to make it grind better and where the drying of the sprouted grain took place to make malt for home-brewed ale.

The evolution of farm-houses, as a result of increased prosperity, has been towards two storeys, slate roofs, separation from the steading, and, in more recent times, the installation of electricity, piped water, and water-borne sanitation.

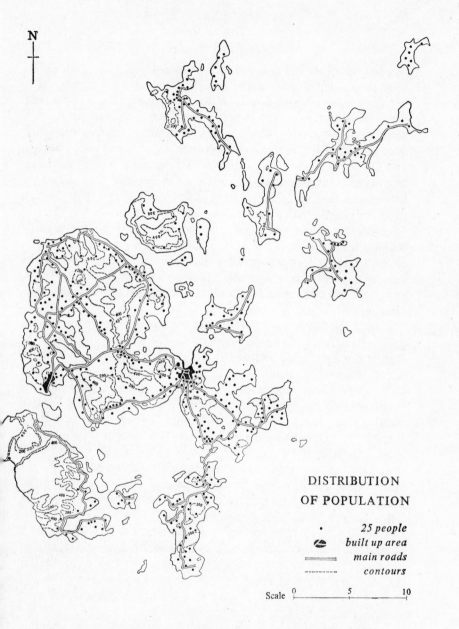

DISTRIBUTION
OF POPULATION

- •   25 people
-      built up area
-      main roads
-      contours

Scale   0   5   10

FIG. 4   The effect of the climate in Orkney is to confine the population almost entirely to the lower ground; very few people live above the 300-foot contour. (This map is based on material provided by Miss Marion Gordon, M.Sc., and drawn by Miss Joan Robertson, both of the Department of Geography, University of Glasgow.)

The Island Economy

The basis of the island economy is overwhelmingly agricultural. We have seen that there are many natural advantages for farming. The extent of these advantages can be judged by comparing Orkney with other counties. The area of Orkney is not great—it comes only twenty-second among the thirty-three counties of Scotland. On the other hand, only ten Scottish counties have more arable area than rough grazings, and Orkney is one of them, with a ratio of three parts crops and grass to two parts rough grazing—the same as for Renfrewshire and only a little poorer than six other counties. Only Fife (8:1) and West Lothian (6:1) have higher ratios among these ten counties.

Conditions favour grass, oats, and roots, and these are fed to cattle with such success that Orkney, which has only 1 per cent of the land of Scotland (but 2·3 per cent of the tillage) produces 4·6 per cent of the beef cattle: indeed only four other counties, Aberdeen, Banff, Angus, and Perth, produce more beef and all of them are larger in area than Orkney.

During the last war, at government request, Orkney went over to milk production, but with the departure of the servicemen in 1946 the market for liquid milk virtually disappeared. To absorb the surplus, cheese was made in quantity, in the style of the traditional farm-house cheese. The old-style cheeses varied enormously in quality, but the best were very good and modern standardised methods have brought all of the output up to this high level, and Orkney cheese now has a national reputation and is a profitable product.

An important characteristic of the typical Orkney farm is its small size, averaging 42 acres, which means that it can be worked by the family without hired labour. On the other hand, to achieve a reasonable income such a small unit must be worked as intensively as possible. Thus Orkney has a high degree of mechanisation, alike in tractors, farm machinery, and motor transport for farm families. Sheep are a characteristically extensive way of using land, cattle intensive, so that the ratio of sheep to cattle is a significant farm index. For Orkney it is 3:2, the same as for Aberdeenshire. Scotland as a whole has 4 sheep to every 1 cattle beast and the crofting counties 9:1. Sutherland, the most extensive of all, has a ratio of no less than 21:1.

Another sign of the willingness to expend much labour and attention on little land in Orkney is poultry-keeping. No doubt the climate is suitable and poultry formerly ate up a proportion of the oat-crop, but transport difficulties hinder both the export of eggs and the import of feeding stuff. In spite of this the poultry industry of Orkney has grown

The Earl's Palace, Kirkwall

A farm scene near Dounby

Aberdeen-Angus, basis of Orkney's prosperity (note tether)

in the last thirty years to near premier position in Scotland, with an egg production topping the £1 million mark until recently, when lower egg prices have made poultry less profitable.

Position, structure, topography, and climate offer in Orkney a reasonable habitat for man. Throughout the centuries the ebb and flow of history has been such as to permit and often encourage him to take advantage of this, so that now, in the second half of the twentieth century, Orkney enjoys its share of the affluence of modern society. This is particularly satisfying because high latitude and long transport routes might suggest that poverty and difficulty would be the rule. Success in the face of difficulty is exhilarating, and not the least characteristic feature of Orkney is the high morale of its people.

13

CLIMATE AND GENERAL WEATHER FEATURES

PRESENT-DAY weather surveying is made possible by the pioneering efforts of a long line of workers and writers in this field. The first of these in Orkney was the Rev. Charles Clouston, minister of Sandwick parish, who in 1827 began a series of systematic weather observations, his only instruments being wet and dry bulb thermometers. A barometer was added in 1839 and two years later a rain gauge. Self-recording maximum and minimum thermometers were acquired in 1856, to be followed in later years by an anemometer (wind-speed recorder) and a sunshine recorder. Subsequent observers and writers, of whom Magnus Spence, schoolmaster in Deerness and author of *Flora Orcadensis* is the best known, have kept records in Deerness, Kirkwall, and Stenness. In more recent times the staff of Grimsetter Meteorological Office at Kirkwall aerodrome and the Leiths of Stenness have provided very interesting and informative data.

Though all records coming from reliable sources and from instruments of approved pattern relate to the mainland of Orkney, it may be assumed that, for the smaller islands of the group, eastern exposures will conform closely to the East Mainland including Kirkwall, and western exposures to Stenness in the West Mainland, with appropriate variations. All conclusions may be interpreted in this fashion for the whole group.

General Features

Orkney shares the maritime climate enjoyed by the whole of Great Britain: in fact, many would say that Orkney has a lion's share of it. From the air and over the sea we are acutely aware of the constant movement of the sea in great tidal sweeps around our islands. The flood-tide brings in the westerly Atlantic Stream. This relatively warm Gulf Stream Drift has a very significant influence on our weather. It is not a steady current from the south-west, but is subject to considerable variation in speed of advance and temperature. Modern theory shows that it ripples across the North Atlantic to our shores in much the same fashion as the south-west airstream which brings warm and damp air over Britain from time to time.

On our eastern seaboard much cooler North Sea tidal currents flow in round Orkney from the south-east during the ebb. The North Sea tides cause sea-mist or fog to form readily in large patches when the dew-point of the air is equal to, or above, that of the sea temperature. We are most aware of this weather feature when the wind is blowing from a south-easterly point and during the ebb-tide. You may hear such mist or fog referred to as the North Sea haar.

Another interesting sea feature, which has had considerable effect on our winter weather during the past decade or so, has been the upwelling round the Hebrides of warmer sea water direct from the Mediterranean. This does not happen every year, and follows no set pattern. How, you may ask, can this water direct from the Mediterranean possibly reach the Hebrides and be separately identified there? It appears that a surface current from the Atlantic flows eastwards through the Straits of Gibraltar. To compensate, there is an outflow below this Atlantic stream of warm Mediterranean water of very high salt content, some of which follows a path north along the edge of the European Continental Shelf and finally, in certain years, upwells over the edge of the Shelf in the region of the Hebrides, mixing as it goes with the North Atlantic Drift, and raising the temperature of the surface waters a degree or two. This Mediterranean water is identified by the type of plankton life which it contains, and especially mild winter seasons result when it reaches our shores.

Our climate in the past has been subject to quite marked variations, in which changes extending over several decades have been super-imposed on a general, though very gradual, warming-up since the close of the last major Ice Age, approximately 10,000 years ago. Within comparatively recent times it appears that cold epochs have coincided roughly with world-wide waves of more intense volcanic activity. There was one such period in the early Iron Age, about 500 B.C., and a second was the 'Little Ice Age' of A.D. 1500–1800. We must not assume that volcanic activity is the only cause of 'Little Ice Ages' but it is part of the answer. In Britain our weather, with capricious variations, started to warm up again progressively from 1850 until about 1940. Similar changes have been noticeable in the Arctic, where permanent ice coverage has decreased and glaciers have retreated. Since 1940 we have experienced a levelling off and now it seems likely that we are in for another dip. This has shown itself already in the Arctic and to a lesser extent in Britain. In recent years there has been a marked increase in volcanic activity: in 1957 eruptions near the Azores extending over the Atlantic Ridge below the sea; in 1961 a flare-up at Tristan-da-Cunha; and in 1963 two new volcanic islands rising out of the sea off Iceland. This latest volcano may well have a profound effect on our weather if the eruption is prolonged. Volcanic dust, projected up through the weather section of the atmosphere—the troposphere—to a height of some 30,000 feet, acts as a part curtain in cutting off the sun's radiation from the earth's surface, and provides an abundant supply of small particles as nuclei on which water droplets can readily form. It is, however, likely that a dip now will only be a climatic phase, and that we can expect a further warming up when it is over.

Orkney Weather

Orkney is open to the force of frequent stormy winds, being often in, or near, the path of the centres of deep depressions (areas of low barometric pressure) moving over the British Isles from the Atlantic. This factor forms the chief difference between Orkney weather and that of the mainland of Scotland. In building, in farming, in gardening —no matter what the activity—one must ever plan with the possibility of high winds in mind. The average annual wind speed varies from 25 m.p.h. at 500 feet on Costa Head to 23 m.p.h. at 430 feet in the west Mainland, and 15 m.p.h. at 130 feet in the east Mainland. This compares with an average annual speed of rather less than 15 m.p.h. in south-west Scotland, where strong winds are also frequent. In Orkney winds from the south are as frequent as from the west; winds from the south-east are almost as frequent; and winds from a northerly point are rather persistent in certain years and spoil our early summer period. Cattle wintering inside come out in the spring, a brief season here, and all too soon are exposed to 'the gab of May' or 'the coo quak' o' May', a period of dry cool weather and grey skies.

Our worst hurricane in living memory occurred in 1952, in mid-January. In 1953 we had our full share of the North Sea Hurricane, which was almost as severe, at the end of January. Since then we have had what might best be described as 'near misses', as in January, 1962, when gales caused damage as far afield as Sheffield and Hamburg, and gusts of up to 177 m.p.h. were recorded in Shetland. It is interesting to recall some of the effects of our 1952 hurricane. The evening of January 14th was fine when Orkney folk went to bed, but the early hours of the 15th were some of the most alarming ever experienced in the islands. By 5.30 a.m. the wind had reached a peak velocity of 135 m.p.h. as it veered from south-west to west. When daylight came Orkney was littered with the materials of broken buildings; countless telephone wires were down in tangled confusion; electricity supplies throughout the Mainland were cut off and roads were partially blocked with the sheaves from a thousand scattered cornstacks. At Howe, near Stromness, a two-hundredweight lump of concrete was blown through a new byre door fifty feet away. At Clestrain, in Stronsay, it was almost as though a bomb had struck the farm buildings, none escaping damage, and some being razed to the ground. A henhouse in Harray smashed its way into a wooden bungalow. It was estimated that Orkney had suffered losses amounting to over half a million pounds. More than eight hundred buildings were destroyed, and 7,000 poultry houses disappeared, together with 86,000 birds. The damage was repaired and life soon became normal again.

Rainfall

The annual amount of rainfall is not high, though rain falls on just over half the days of the year. The figure often quoted for the average annual rainfall in Orkney, from the records of Magnus Spence, Deerness, is 36·65 inches, but, as we shall see, the West Mainland of Orkney is slightly wetter than the East, and in recent years there has been a significant increase of approximately 3 inches, this increase showing over the East Mainland only after 1950.

Early records of the Rev. Charles Clouston of Sandwick, probably the second oldest in Scotland, gave an average figure of 37·24 inches for the years from 1841 to 1880. His work has been continued in recent times by Peter Leith, farmer at Appiehouse, Stenness, with instruments of standard pattern, and the average for 1943 to 1962 is 39·91 inches, an increase of 2·67 inches.

Combining all records from Deerness, Kirkwall, and Grimsetter, from 1881 to 1950, the average annual rainfall was 36·01 inches, but thereafter the figure at Grimsetter for five years from 1951 to 1955 showed an increase of 3·50 inches, and in 1962—a 'record' year nearly everywhere—the rainfall was 41·27 inches. In Stenness in 1962 it amounted to 46·15 inches. However 1963 was a complete contrast, being a very dry year.

In comparison the average annual rainfall in Moray, Edinburgh, and the south coast of England is from 26 to 28 inches, in south-west Scotland from 45 to 50 inches, and in certain parts of the western Highlands over 100 inches.

Snowfalls are less frequent in Orkney than elsewhere in the north, but more frequent than in the south of Scotland. At Deerness between 1916 and 1935 snow fell on an average of 45·8 days annually, including

7 days in each of the months of December, January, February, and April, and 8 days in March. The number of days when snow is actually lying is the much smaller annual figure of 14. In the Highlands it lies on 55 to 60 days, in Aberdeenshire inland up to 30 days, in south and west Scotland on 6 to 12 days, and on the south coast of England only 3 days. However 1963 markedly failed to conform with this pattern; the duration of snow lying in the south of England was quite exceptional and disrupted life there, while Orkney was singularly free from long-lying snow.

Sunshine and Frost

April, May, and June are, as a rule, our sunniest months, and December the most gloomy, though hours of sunshine vary greatly in different districts and from year to year. Some of our records are:

Deerness: 1881–1907	Average annual hours of sunshine=1,177
	Hours during December vary from 6 to 39
	Hours during June vary from 86 to 238
Kirkwall: 1921–44	Average annual hours of sunshine=1,155
	Average hours for December = 23
	Average hours for June = 158
Grimsetter: 1963	Total hours of sunshine =1,160
Stenness: 1963	Total hours of sunshine =1,066

From these figures it is likely that the East Mainland is slightly more sunny than the West, or at least than most places in the West Mainland. Birsay and Evie may well differ in this respect. Overall, we rather lack sunshine, for Moray has an annual average of 1,290 hours, south-west Scotland about 1,320, and the south coast of England about 1,800.

However, such is the effect of the sea, which acts as our best heat reservoir, that Orkney winter temperatures are similar to those in south-west Scotland, being on an average 41°F. in December and 40°F. in January. Even in July the figure for Orkney, 54°F., is only 3·5°F. less than that for the southern area. From 1860 to 1908 our minimum temperature in January was 7·8°F. and our maximum in July was 76°F., but in recent years the highest reading has just topped 70°F., e.g. at Stenness in 1963 the peak was 71°F. on 30 July.

The growing season is reckoned as the time between the first day in spring on which mean air temperature rises to 42°F., and the first day in autumn on which air temperature fails to reach 42°F. In Orkney this amounts to about 230 days each year. This period is about a month shorter than in south-west Scotland.

There are fewer severe or continuous spells of frost in Orkney than in other parts of the north of Scotland, but frost occurs in some years as frequently in April as in December, and, over five recent years at Grimsetter, August was the only frost-free month in every year.

In an interesting experiment now being carried out at Stenness, soil temperatures at varying depths of 2 inches to 12 inches below grass level are being recorded systematically. Results obtained on 12 January, 1963, during a keen frost, are as follows:

Temperature of air   = 8·9°F.
Grass minimum (thermometer lying on grass)= 5·9°F.
At 4 inches below ground level, temperature =32·8°F.
At 12 inches below ground level, temperature=34·9°F.

Hence our remote ancestors who dug themselves homes below ground level had at least one sound reason for their choice of domicile, and only in recent times are we learning how to keep our houses as free from frost as were the 'Picts' houses'.

The Orcadian Old Red Sandstone

UNLIKE Shetland, where the geological structure is fairly complex, the rock formations in Orkney are relatively simple in pattern and in this respect resemble the rocks of Caithness on the other side of the Pentland Firth.

Sandstones and flagstones are the main rock types in Orkney. Granitic and schistose rocks, which occur at Graemsay, Stromness, and Yesnaby, are the basement rocks, representing parts of the old land surface on which the sediments which on compaction produced these sandstones and flagstones were originally deposited. There are a few occurrences of basaltic lava, presumably extruded from minor local volcanoes, and a much larger number of intrusive dykes which have penetrated the sedimentary rocks and which may be readily recognised from the typically straight-walled appearance which gives rise to their name.

The sedimentary rocks, particularly the flagstones, are well-bedded. The closely spaced bedding planes or lamination of the flagstones created a great demand for them in the past as paving stones, roofing material, and vertical fencing slabs. These rocks show almost perfect geometrical patterns of joints along which separation on a minute scale divides the rocks into rectangular slabs which may be readily extracted from the quarry face. The influence of joints on the natural sculpture of prominent coastal features is also very marked.

In terms of Historical Geology, the sedimentary rocks of Orkney are referred to the Devonian system which, in the type locality of Devon and Cornwall, is characterised by rocks originally deposited as sediments in the sea. In Orkney, however, the deposits were laid down in fresh-water lagoons and mountain lakes. These non-marine deposits, generally red in colour, consist largely of sandstone and are known as the Old Red Sandstone, with an estimated age of about 400 million years. The Old Red Sandstone consists of three main divisions known as the Lower, Middle, and Upper, but in Orkney the Lower Old Red Sandstone is absent.

The Middle Old Red Sandstone of Orkney has a maximum thickness of over 14,000 feet of sandstones and flagstones. There are three main sub-divisions known as the Stromness Beds, the Rousay Beds, and the Eday Beds, occurring in that order of superposition and named after the localities in which each sub-division is typically developed. The Stromness Beds, the lowest in the sequence, have been laid down on the worn surface of the much older rocks of the Granite-schist complex which outcrop in the Stromness neighbourhood.

The Upper Old Red Sandstone sediments have been laid down in turn on the weathered surface of the Middle Old Red Sandstone. The Upper Old Red Sandstone is restricted to the island of Hoy and is made up of 3,500 feet of Hoy Sandstone overlying 400 feet of rock derived from material discharged from volcanoes which were active before the deposition of the sandstone. The red and yellow sandstones of Hoy have given rise to the steep but well-rounded hills which make such a marked contrast with the low relief of the rest of Orkney. The summit of the Ward Hill of Hoy at 1,565 feet above sea-level is the highest point in Orkney.

The dykes, of which there are more than two hundred, are of much more recent date than the sediments they have penetrated, but it is difficult to give an estimate of their age.

Fish Beds

For well over a century the remains of the primitive fish found in varying states of preservation in the sedimentary rocks, and especially the flagstones, of Orkney, have been the subject of scientific study by the foremost authorities in this particular field of research, including that well-known investigator Hugh Miller. Apart from one group, those fish have no known living representatives or descendants.

The rock foundation in which the fossil fish are found in notable concentration are referred to as 'fish beds'. The area most prolific in these fish remains is the west Mainland, where they are mostly confined to the Stromness Flags and particularly to the rocks near to what is regarded as the junction of the Middle and Upper Stromness Flags. In the west Mainland these 'fish beds' occur in a series of slightly curved belts trending roughly north and south. Fish beds of much lesser extent occur in the island of Rousay, in the Rousay Flags which are younger than the Stromness Flags.

Igneous Rocks and Structures

The term igneous (Latin: *ignis*—fire) is applied to rocks which have been solidified from a mass of originally molten material known as a *magma*. The composition of the magma and the conditions under which the solidification takes place determine the chemical composition, the mineral content, the texture of the rock, and the shape it may finally assume.

The granite of the Stromness neighbourhood has solidified at a great depth, and under intense pressure, in the earth's crust. It is exposed at the surface today because the immense thickness of cover of overlying rocks has been partially removed by wind, rain, and frost.

The igneous rocks known as dykes and sills solidified much nearer the surface under conditions of much lower temperature and pressure and differ considerably in volume, texture, and structural pattern from the granite masses.

The dykes may pierce great thicknesses of overlying rocks before solidifying. The sills, as the name suggests, are extensive, flat tabular bodies. They, as distinct from dykes, tend to insinuate themselves along bedding planes or other easily opened passages in the overlying rocks.

The dykes and sills are much younger than the sandstones and flagstones which they have intruded. There are over two hundred dykes in Orkney varying in width from a few inches to several feet. Along the Orkney coastline, particularly on the west coast of the Mainland, they form vertical or nearly vertical wall-like structures, mostly standing slightly above the rocks which they have penetrated and so are reasonably easy to detect. Many of the dykes are aligned in an east by north direction.

In Orkney the one known intrusion with the characteristic structure of a sill occurs at the base of the cliffs which form the eastern face of the Kame of Hoy, and penetrates beds of Lower Stromness age. The writer, with the assistance of a friend with intimate knowledge of the locality and the tides, succeeded in collecting specimens of the rock from a cave which breaches the cliff and to which access by a small boat is possible only at the infrequent coincidence of suitable tides and good weather conditions.

The volcanic rocks, of which there are a moderate number of types in Orkney, have mostly been poured out at the earth's surface as molten lava from either volcanic cones or long narrow fissures. The remainder are principally the rocks known as tuff, or bedded ash, and agglomerate, which are respectively the consolidated forms of the very fine material and the large fragments, blown out of the crater during eruption.

Signs of former local volcanic activity are to be seen in different parts of Orkney. One of the best known is the lava flow at the base of the Old Man o' Hoy. Here the lava overlies the Stromness Flags of Middle Old Red Sandstone age and is in turn overlain by 450 feet of well-bedded sandstone of Upper Old Red Sandstone age, clearly indicating that the eruption took place in the interval between the compaction of the Stromness Flags and the deposition of the sediments which gave rise to the Upper Old Red Sandstone.

Glacial Phenomena

Of comparatively recent geological date are the deposits left by glaciers on the Orkney landscape. These reminders of the former presence of glaciers take the form of boulder clay, finely pulverised rock material containing rock boulders, representing the ground moraines of ice-sheets left behind when the ice retreated or melted. There are also the materials of the moraines which mark the sites of the ends and flanks of glaciers. In addition there are the sands and gravels deposited by the melt-water streams from glaciers. The comprehensive name 'drift' is applied to all types of glacial deposits.

Although there is a fairly widespread mantle of drift in Orkney its distribution is rather irregular and its thickness is very variable.

Many of the boulders in the boulder clay are not of local origin: these erratics, as they are called, have apparently been carried by ice from other regions and their presence furnishes a clue to the probable direction of movement of the ice. The erosive action of the moving glacier whose base is armed with hard rocks is responsible for the shallow grooving on the rock surfaces they traverse, now visible as series of parallel lines known as 'glacial striae' which give a fair indication of the course of the ice.

The transport of local rocks by ice has produced in Orkney an interesting transition from red and purple clay and rock debris in the east, where the boulders have been derived from the red sandstones of Eday, to a yellowish clayey rubble in the west where the rocks have been taken from the Rousay and Stromness beds.

Subsequent to the disappearance of the ice there was a notable difference between Orkney and the greater part of the rest of Scotland in their respective reactions to adjustments in sea-level. Whilst the west of Scotland shows uplift by the presence of raised beaches at elevations ranging from 25 feet to 100 feet or more above present sea-level, Orkney has apparently experienced corresponding depressions but not necessarily to the same vertical extent. This is revealed in Orkney by the presence of peaty matter, remains of trees and other vegetation, and former high-level storm beaches, now below high-water mark and covered with the materials of the present beach.

Unconsolidated Deposits

Peat, despite its absence of stony characteristics, is of considerable geological interest, and as the result of compression and compaction may, and frequently does, assume the appearance of a stratified deposit. In many parts of the world, as the result of this process operating over long periods in geological history, the peat has eventually been converted into coals of varying rank. In Orkney, however, the peat is of very recent geological age, post-dating the glacial deposits, and still ranks as peat although it has been cut extensively as a source of solid fuel.

Shell sand is another unconsolidated deposit which occurs on most of the Orkney beaches and occasionally inland as accumulations of wind-borne material. As the name implies it consists essentially of very small fragments of sea-shells rich in carbonate of calcium. There are many quite considerable deposits in the west Mainland and some in the North Isles, particularly in Sanday and Westray. These concentrations are valuable sources of lime in Orkney and the material has been largely used for agricultural purposes.

Two Distinctive Features

It has been already indicated that the geology of Orkney is fairly simple and uncomplicated as far as rock types and structures are concerned. For this reason it has not the same attraction for geologists as Shetland and the north-west Highlands of Scotland. However, there is one outstanding compensating feature, for which the more interesting but less productive areas would willingly exchange their exciting geological problems, namely, the impressive acreage of land of high agricultural and pastoral value in Orkney, based on the regular well-bedded flagstones with their very useful natural content of lime.

Also, Orkney is undoubtedly pre-eminent in the natural rock sculpture to be seen in such great variety round its coasts. These impressive sea-scapes are largely due to geological agencies other than those to which reference has already been made.

The sea in stormy weather acts as a gigantic water-hammer, beating at the rocks, compressing the air in all crevices and cavities, and creating a vacuum on withdrawal, as a result of which huge blocks are blown out by back pressure. The destructive impact of breakers is very considerable. The pressure exerted by Atlantic waves, for example, averages about a quarter of a ton per square foot in the summer, and a ton per square foot in the winter, whilst in storms it may be as much as three tons.

Coastal features are generally produced by the destructive action of the sea, operating on rock formations which are either faulted or jointed. Joints develop in rocks from a number of causes, the two most important of which are earth-movement and shrinkage during consolidation. Such divisional planes help in quarrying operations and the sea makes full use of this natural aid in extraction of rock material.

Closely-spaced parallel dykes also facilitate the removal of intervening rock along the planes of contact with the dykes. This is admirably shown at the well-known Hole o' Rowe, on the south side of the Bay of Skaill, where a pair of north-east dykes form the vertical walls of the sea-cave.

The characteristic products of marine erosion most frequently developed in Orkney are the long narrow inlets of the sea known as geos, sea-caves, blowholes or gloups, sea-arches, and sea-stacks.

The sea-cave results from the removal of rock along the line of fault planes, joints, or parallel dykes. There are many sea-caves along the Orkney coastline, notably in the Yesnaby area. The geos appear to be the residual features of sea-caves whose roofs have collapsed. The blow-hole or gloup, a local name now accepted by some writers, is a natural chimney or vertical shaft in a sea-cave communicating with the surface at some distance inland from the edge of the cliff. There are excellent examples of gloups in Deerness, Swona, Rousay and the previously mentioned Hole o' Rowe in Sandwick.

When two sea-caves on opposite sides of a narrow headland unite, a natural arch is produced. It may persist as such for a time but eventually the arch falls and the seaward of the headland remains as an isolated sea-stack. On Orkney waters there are several of these, some of which are called 'castles'. The best known of them all, and certainly the most frequently pointed out, is the Old Man o' Hoy, a 450-feet-high column of well-bedded Upper Old Red Sandstone resting on lava rock ejected from a local volcano some time before the deposition of the sandstone.

Economic Geology

Apart from the working of peat for fuel, flagstones for roofing-slates, road metal, building stone, fencing slabs, shell sand for agricultural lime, and, of course, the soil for pasturage and arable land, Orkney has little history of exploitation of its native mineral resources, largely, it would appear, because of their sporadic occurrence in disappointingly small bulk.

There are records of lead being worked in South Ronaldsay, Hoy, Graemsay, and Stromness where the opening into the old lead mine was a familiar feature to the youth of Stromness in the early part of this century when it served as an improvised shelter for the bathers at

Warbeth. All these workings, however, had closed down before the end of the eighteenth century.

Copper ore was worked in the early part of the eighteenth century at Wha Taing in Burray, and in Rousay may be seen the filled-in shafts of what were, presumably, trial workings for copper. Copper minerals in minor amounts have also been reported in Yesnaby.

Ores of both iron and manganese were worked in the latter half of the eighteenth century in the island of Hoy. The manganese ore was won from an ore-body situated 200 feet below the top of a 900-foot cliff.

All these workings have long since been abandoned and there is little likelihood of renewal of operations in any of the metalliferous ores in Orkney.

15

BIRD LIFE IN THE ISLANDS

MANY orders and families of land and water birds are represented in Orkney, either as residents or as visitors. When we think of them in systematic form, it is convenient to begin with the primitive birds, the Divers, and work through intermediate groups up to the more advanced species, the Sparrows. This is in accordance with the Wetmore classification, which has been widely adopted since about 1950.

The Divers and Grebes are water birds, represented by two somewhat scarce breeding species in the Red-throated Diver and the Slavonian Grebe. Among the mainly oceanic Petrels and Shearwaters we have one very common nester, the Fulmar, and two more scarce and rather obscure nesters, the Stormy Petrel and the Manx Shearwater. Gannets and Cormorants are large and familiar sea birds. While Cormorants and Shags are fairly common everywhere, the sole nesting place of the Gannet in Orkney is Sule Stack (a rock thirty miles west from Hoy, and near Sule Skerry), where there is a large colony. In the next three groups, Herons, Spoonbills, and Ibises, we have only one member, the Common Heron, which is well known. The Ducks, Geese, and Swans are well represented by many nesting and wintering species.

There are only four species of Raptors (i.e. Hawks, Eagles, and Falcons) that nest regularly in Orkney—the Peregrine, Merlin, Kestrel, and Hen Harrier. The latter owes to Orkney its survival as a British bird, because here it weathered the storm of persecution after the turn of the century. The only native game bird is the Red Grouse, though the Quail has nested occasionally. Cranes are almost unknown in Orkney, but Craiks, Rails, and Coots are represented by the Corncrake, Waterhen, and Coot and also by the rarer Water Rail. The Waders are a numerous group comprising Oystercatchers, Plovers, Curlews, Godwits, Shanks, Sandpipers, Snipe, and Phalarope. They include residents, summer and winter visitors, and passage migrants and often frequent sea and loch shores, sometimes in big flocks.

Another well-known group is made up of Skuas, Gulls, and Terns. Skuas are relatively scarce, while some of the Gulls are very numerous.

Two species of Skua, six Gulls and three Terns nest regularly and a few others occur mainly as winter visitors or passage migrants. The colonial, cliff-nesting Auks are a familiar feature of our rocky shores in summer. Four species that nest are the Common Guillemot, Black Guillemot, Razorbill, and Puffin: the latter nests in great numbers on Sule Skerry. The smallest of this distinctive black-and-white group, the Little Auk, is a winter visitor. Three species of Cuckoo have been observed but only the Common Cuckoo is well known. Among the Owls, the Short-eared is common, and although the Long-eared Owl nests in very small numbers it is better known as a winter visitor. Others such as the Snowy Owl are rarely seen. Then there are a number of small orders that do not occur at all regularly and include Nightjars, Kingfishers, Rollers, Hoopoes, and Woodpeckers. Of these the Great Spotted Woodpecker is the commonest visitant. The Hirundines that can be seen in small numbers are Swift, Swallow, House Martin, and Sand Martin, of which only the Swallow nests fairly regularly. Orioles are but rarely observed, but the Crow family is familiar enough, from the large Raven to the perky Jackdaw: four species are resident nesters. Lastly come the small Passerines or Perchers. They make up the most numerous group of all and include all our song-birds: Larks, Thrushes, Chats, Warblers, Pipits, Finches, Buntings, and Sparrows. Several species nest with us and there is a long list of visitors or migrants.

A Second Method of Classification

It has been customary also to classify our bird population by reference to their way of life: they may be *residents, summer visitors, winter visitors, passage migrants, occasional visitors, wanderers, and rare visitors.* This method, neat and tidy as it appears, can lead to some confusion because nature does not always conform to rigid divisions, and some species can equally well be placed in two or even three categories, e.g., the Mallard or Wild Duck. Some individuals are residents in Orkney, others are winter visitors from farther north, while a third group are passage migrants, passing through Orkney on their way south in autumn, or north in spring. Again, of a species mainly winter visitors, a few individuals will occasionally stay throughout the summer. Well-known summer visitors such as the Arctic Tern and the Dunlin or Plover Page come here to nest, but some of their fellows carry on farther north for the same purpose—so we think of them as being summer visitors, or summer residents on the one hand and passage migrants on the other.

All these groups fall into two main divisions—those that breed here, and those that do not. Of the breeders, over one half are residents and

A fossil fish from Stromness flags

Flagstones raised by the sea, West Shore, Stromness

The Hole o' Rowe, Sandwick, showing marine erosion along two

The Gault of Vaurby, Sandwick

the remainder mainly summer visitors. The average number of species in any one year is around 85, but the total of those that have nested during the present century is about 100. A few have nested on one or two occasions only. These have been either northern or Arctic species which normally winter here, such as the Long-tailed Duck, or southern or continental birds which are normally passage migrants such as the Whitethroat and Blackcap. The non-breeders are composed of winter visitors, passage migrants, and irregular or rare visitors. Although Orkney does lack many of the small birds, including the complete Tit family, it has a list of over 270 species of which about a third nest more or less regularly.

This number is perhaps greater than we might expect in view of our northern latitude, but the islands have a good geographical position, lying off the northern tip of Britain between the Atlantic and the North Sea. Further they provide a fairly wide choice of habitats—places where a variety of species may each find its requirements for nesting, feeding, and resting: fine sea-cliffs where large numbers of sea birds nest: sandy bays and muddy estuaries that provide feeding places for many wading birds and ducks: marshes, both salt and fresh: fresh-water lochs and pools, some with suitable nesting islands and reedy margins: various types of moorland and heather hills: even mountainous terrain with inland cliffs. A suitable proportion of the land is rich and cultivated: it not only provides crops, but a large number of insects, grubs, and worms on which so many kinds of birds feed. The few small plantations and many gardens with trees are much appreciated by small passerines and other tree-nesting species. There are also many (mainly dwarf) willow bushes and a quantity of gorse, sometimes in the form of hedges that afford good cover for small birds. However, it must not be thought that Orkney has more species of nesting birds than other parts of the British Isles.

Losses and Gains in Bird Populations

Changes in bird populations are continually taking place, some of a spectacular nature, others hardly noticeable. Over the years Orkney has lost some species and gained others, while the status of many more have changed. Often these changes are caused by the activities of man. Direct persecution was responsible for the extinction of the large and flightless Great Auk. The last one to be seen in Orkney was shot in 1813. Both the Golden Eagle and the White-tailed Eagle or Erne were driven out of Orkney in the second half of the nineteenth century by shooting and persistent nest robbing. The loss of the Whooper Swan as a breeding species—it still comes regularly as a winter visitor—was brought about in a different way, by being ousted by the more pugnacious semi-domesticated Mute Swan introduced by man early in the nineteenth century. Two species which have benefited from man's activities are the Rook and Wood-pigeon. They came in to take advantage of the newly established tree plantations about the same time as the Eagles were going out. Perhaps the most spectacular increase has been the spread of the Fulmar or Mallimack around the northern coasts of Britain. It nested in Orkney for the first time about 1900 and is now one of the commonest cliff-nesting birds. The increase of the Fulmar has been attributed to some extent to the expansion of the fishing industry, as fish offal thrown overboard in greater quantities has given them a new and readily accessible food supply.

The most notable decline has been that of the Corncrake or Land Rail, which was a very common summer bird until about thirty years ago, and is now quite scarce. For this haymaking and modern grass-management machinery has been held responsible, but the evidence is by no means conclusive. Other birds that have decreased within the same period are the Lapwing, Golden Plover, Corn Bunting, and Pied Wagtail: the Greater Black-backed Gull, Great Skua, Curlew, Oyster-catcher, and Reed Bunting have all increased. There are many smaller fluctuations, chiefly affecting species at the fringe of their range. About 1940 Orkney lost the Dipper as a breeding bird, and in 1960 gained the Tree Sparrow. On the danger list is that dainty swimming wader, the Red-necked Phalarope. Always scarce, it has dwindled in numbers in recent years and may soon disappear altogether. The reason for this decline is not properly known, but may well be some environmental or climatic change. The noble Peregrine Falcon, which one is apt to think secure in its rocky fastness, has also fallen on bad times: numbers have slumped sadly all over Britain: birds have failed to lay eggs and eggs have failed to hatch. The trouble is believed to be caused by the use of certain toxic chemicals in agriculture. So far Orkney has not been badly affected, but there have been some ominous symptoms and the species may be in danger. As losses seem imminent, there are good prospects of at least one gain. The Collared Dove, a small dove allied to the Turtle Dove, has in recent years made a remarkable spread from the Balkans north-westward across Europe. It has already established itself as a nesting bird in parts of the east and north of Scotland and now appears to be resident in Orkney also. Attempts to introduce game birds such as Partridges, Ptarmigans, and Black Grouse have always ended in failure. Pheasants are being tried with some initial success, but are unlikely to live in the wild in such a sparsely wooded place as Orkney.

Adaptations

In some cases a few of our birds, mostly tree- or bush-nesting species, have adapted themselves to types of nesting habitat differing from the normal. Here heather has been found an acceptable substitute where trees and bushes are lacking. For the Wood-pigeon or Ring Dove food was no problem but there was a distributional scarcity of nesting trees. So the first pair tried nesting among tall heather a few years prior to 1940. The experiment was a success and the habit soon spread to a number of other suitable places. In the early 1940s that beautiful little hovering hawk, the Kestrel, also took to the heather. Until then it had used typical nest sites on cliffs, quarries, and, rarely, in trees. Nesting on the ground, among the roots of tall luxuriant heather and in holes beneath, proved to be very successful and again the adaptation became widespread. Other species that are not traditional heather nesters frequently do so in Orkney. These include the Shelduck or Sly Goose, Blackbird, Song Thrush or Mavis, Starling and on at least one occasion the Sedge Warbler. Herons usually nest colonially in tall trees, but in Orkney and in one or two places in the north of Scotland they nest on sea cliffs.

Migration

In its simplest form migration is a regular seasonal movement, northwards in spring and southwards in autumn. The birds gain an advantage both ways—the long daylight of northern summers, which appears to be essential for the rearing of their young, and the milder southern climate in which to overwinter. Many of our nesting birds are migrants or summer visitors, and even some of our resident birds make limited local movements from breeding ground to winter feeding ground, such as Curlews from moorland to shore. Then, because our islands straddle some of the migration routes, they are visited by a more transient group of birds, the passage migrants which may stop briefly to feed and rest *en route* to their breeding or winter quarters as the case may be. The spring passage is the more colourful with the birds resplendent in their breeding plumage, but the autumn passage is of much greater volume, the ranks of the breeders then being swelled by the young of the year. Migration is often affected by weather conditions. The birds may lose their way in fog, or get blown off course by adverse winds. This has added considerably to our list of rare visitors, mainly from continental Europe, but also from America. From 1959 to 1963 there were seven such species—Little Egret, Night Heron, Red-footed Falcon, Collared Dove (first recorded in 1962), Great Spotted Cuckoo, American Robin, and Collared Flycatcher.

Conservation

Great advances have been made in our knowledge of bird life within the last twenty-five years. Many books have been written, based on observation and experiment, and films and sound recordings have been made available to all through radio and television. This has led to increased interest and concern for the welfare of the bird population, constantly threatened by human activities, such as shooting, taking eggs, and destroying nests. It is usually the rarer birds which suffer most.

The practice of taking wild birds' eggs for food has decreased, and although numerous species, as the big gulls, can well withstand such human predation, it is indefensible to rob a Lapwing's nest, since the bird is becoming increasingly scarce. The birds of prey have suffered persecution most of all, and without sound reason. Apart from direct destruction, alterations in the countryside, ploughing out of moorland, draining of marshes, burning of heather, tend to limit the birds and destroy their habitats: again, though, the establishment of small plantations of trees has provided shelter and nesting places and an attraction for birds new to our county. An essential requirement for the future is that we should leave enough 'wet lands' in their natural state. With care, and the knowledge we now have, our precious heritage of bird life will be maintained and fostered.

REFERENCES

Rev. James Wallace, *Description of the Isles of Orkney*. Edinburgh, 1693.
Rev. George Low, *Fauna Orcadensis*. Edinburgh, 1775.
T. E. Buckley and J. A. Harvie-Brown, *A vertebrate fauna of the Orkney Islands*. Edinburgh, 1891.
James Omond, *How to know the Orkney Birds*. Kirkwall, 1925.
D. J. Robertson, *Notes from a Bird Sanctuary*. Kirkwall, 1934.

BIRDS THAT BREED OR HAVE BRED IN ORKNEY SINCE 1900
(Classified according to Wetmore)

		Local Names	Status
1	Red-throated Diver	*Rain Goose*	fairly common
2	Little Grebe	*Dabchick*	scarce
3	Storm Petrel		scarce
4	Manx Shearwater	*Lyre*	
5	Fulmar	*Mallimack*	numerous
6	Gannet	*Solan Goose*	colony of *c* 1,000 pairs on Sule Skerry
7	Cormorant	*Hibling*	
8	Shag	*Scarf*	common
9	Heron		one small colony
10	Mallard	*Wild Duck or Stock Duck*	common
11	Teal		fairly common
12	Wigeon		rare
13	Pintail		rare
14	Shoveller		mainly confined to the North Isles
15	Scaup Duck		has bred a few times
16	Tufted Duck		fairly common
17	Pochard		rare
18	Long-tailed Duck	*Calloo*	has bred
19	Common Scoter		has bred a few times recently
20	Eider Duck	*Dunter*	common
21	Red-breasted Merganser	*Sawbill*	common
22	Shelduck	*Sly Goose*	common
23	Mute Swan		common
24	Sparrow Hawk		has bred a few times
25	Hen Harrier	*Gos-haak*	fairly common
26	Peregrine Falcon		rather scarce
27	Merlin		rather scarce
28	Kestrel	*Moosie Haak*	fairly common
29	Red Grouse	*Muir Hen*	fairly common
30	Quail		has bred occasionally
31	Water Rail		rare
32	Corncrake		formerly common—much rarer now
33	Moorhen	*Water Hen*	common
34	Coot		locally scarce
35	Oystercatcher	*Skeldro, Scottie*	common
36	Lapwing	*Teeo, Teeack, Peewit, Peesweep*	common
37	Ringed Plover	*Sinloo, Sandlark*	common
38	Golden Plover		fairly common
39	Common Snipe	*Horse-gowk*	common

		Local Names	*Status*
40	Curlew	*Whaap, Whaup*	common and increasing
41	Black-tailed Godwit		has nested
42	Common Sandpiper	*Boondie*	becoming scarce
43	Redshank		common
44	Greenshank		has nested
45	Dunlin	*Plover Page*	becoming less common
46	Red-necked Phalarope		very rare
47	Arctic Skua	*Scootie Allan*	fairly common locally
48	Great Skua	*Bonxie*	rather scarce
49	Great Black-backed Gull	*Baakie*	common
50	Lesser Black-backed Gull		fairly common
51	Herring Gull	*White Maa*	very common
52	Common Gull	*White Maa*	common
53	Black-headed Gull		common
54	Kittiwake	*Kittiewaako, Kittick*	very numerous on several cliffs
55	Common Tern	*Pickie terno, Ritto, Rittick*	rather scarce
56	Arctic Tern	*Pickie terno, Ritto, Rittick*	common
57	Sandwich Tern		locally common in parts of the North Isles
58	Razorbill	*Cooter-neb*	common
59	Common Guillemot	*Aak*	numerous on several sea-cliffs
60	Black Guillemot	*Tyste*	fairly common
61	Puffin	*Tammie-norrie*	fairly common, large colony on Sule Skerry
62	Rock Dove	*Doo*	common
63	Wood-pigeon or Ring Dove		fairly common
64	Cuckoo		rare
65	Long-eared Owl		rare
66	Short-eared Owl	*Cattie-face*	fairly common
67	Sky Lark	*Laverock, Laveroo*	common
68	Swallow		rare
69	House Martin		has bred occasionally
70	Raven	*Corbie*	fairly common
71	Hooded Crow	*Craa, Hoodie-craw, Grey-back*	common
72	Rook		common
73	Jackdaw	*Jackie, Kae*	common
74	Wren	*Jenny Wren*	common
75	Dipper		has nested
76	Mistle Thrush		rare
77	Song Thrush	*Mavis*	common
78	Ring Ouzel		has bred
79	Blackbird	*Blackie*	common
80	Wheatear	*Chackie, Stonechat*	fairly common
81	Stonechat		scarce

		Local Names	*Status*
82	Whinchat		has bred
83	Robin	*Robin Redbreast*	scarce
84	Sedge Warbler		scarce
85	Blackcap		has bred
86	Whitethroat		one nesting recorded, in 1941
87	Willow Warbler		scarce
88	Goldcrest		has bred a few times recently, in 1945 and 1962
89	Spotted Flycatcher		scarce
90	Hedge Sparrow or Dunnock		fairly common
91	Meadow Pipit	*Teeting*	common
92	Rock Pipit	*Tang Sparrow, Tang Teeting*	common
93	Pied Wagtail	*Willie Wagtail*	has become rather scarce from about 1935
94	Starling	*Stirling, Strill*	very common
95	Greenfinch		locally fairly common
96	Linnet	*Rose Lintie, Lintie Lintic*	fairly common
97	Twite	*Heather Lintie*	common
98	Chaffinch		fairly common
99	Yellowhammer or Yellow Bunting	*Yellow Yarling*	becoming scarce
100	Corn Bunting	*Skitter Broltie*	becoming scarce
101	Reed Bunting	*Blackcap*	common
102	House Sparrow	*Sprug*	very common
103	Tree Sparrow		has bred since 1960

SOME WINTER VISITORS

Great Northern Diver	Common Scoter	Purple Sandpiper
Slavonian Grebe	Grey Lag Goose	Dunlin
Wigeon	White-fronted Goose	Glaucous Gull
Pintail	Barnacle Goose	Iceland Gull
Scaup Duck	Whooper Swan	Little Auk
Tufted Duck	Golden Plover	Long-eared Owl
Pochard	Turnstone	Fieldfare
Goldeneye Duck	Jack Snipe	Robin
Long-tailed Duck	Woodcock	Snow Bunting
Velvet Scoter	Bar-tailed Godwit	

16

THE MAMMALS OF ORKNEY

1. LAND MAMMALS

The Pygmy Shrew, *Sorex Minutus*

THIS species, the smallest mammal found in Britain, reaches a maximum length of two and a quarter inches from tip of snout to root of tail. Its tail is nearly three-quarters the length of its body, slightly longer than in the case of the Common Shrew, the tail of which is usually half its body length.

In colour it is darkish grey-brown, the winter coat being generally darker than in summer, when there is more of a reddish brown in the colouring. The most distinctive feature of a shrew is its long snout almost like a trunk projecting well beyond its mouth. This trunk is flexible and can be turned in any direction while the animal is reaching for insects, which are its chief food.

It is an inoffensive and useful creature, eating beetles, flies, and all kinds of insects with their larvae and grubs. It has a gland on each flank which gives off a disagreeable odour when it is in danger, this being its sole protection against enemies. This explains why cats leave them uneaten when caught.

Shrews live in ditches, fields, and rough vegetation and may sometimes be seen climbing on grass stems in hunting for insects. They make a nest of dry grass or other herbage, in holes or under stones. The Orkney names are the Rone Mouse and the Sheer Mouse.

The Pygmy Shrew is found in most parts of the Mainland and in at least some of the islands. The writer has handled specimens from Graemsay, Stenness, Holm, and Stromness, and it is said to be found in Westray and South Ronaldsay.

The Hedgehog, *Erinaceus europaeus*

During the past twenty years the hedgehog has firmly established itself as one of our Orkney mammals. There is no mention of its occurrence in Orkney prior to 1870 when, as recorded in Buckley and Harvie-

Brown's *Fauna*, 'a few hedgehogs were brought to Orkney by the sons of Dr Logie, minister of Dirleton, and turned out about 1870'.

Those original introductions may have died out, though it is interesting to note that hedgehogs introduced into Shetland during the second half of the nineteenth century survived and became widely distributed, not only in the Mainland of Shetland but in many of the outlying islands. Its present abundance in Orkney is probably the result of its re-introduction by troops during the 1939–45 war.

In October or November, hedgehogs go into hibernation. In a bank or hedge, or in the peaty banks of such places as the Loons behind Stromness, it builds a warm nest of decayed vegetation in which it lies torpid till March. The nest is so constructed that the animal is entirely enwound in a cosy blanket of grass which provides adequate warmth and keeps out the frost.

In spring, as the temperature rises, the hedgehog awakens out of its winter sleep to resume its normal life throughout the summer and autumn. It hunts mainly by night, though it may sometimes be seen during the day, and in the course of a night's hunting it may travel as far as a mile or two from its nest.

Its hearing is sensitive. To certain sounds it reacts quickly by erecting its spines, even when in its winter sleep. The spines are its natural protection. They are about $\frac{3}{4}$ of an inch long and project outwards in all directions when the animal curls itself defensively into a ball. This reaction to dangerous sounds probably explains why hedgehogs are frequently found crushed by traffic on the roads in areas where they are common. This is now frequently seen on the Kirkwall-Stromness road.

Bats

Of the twelve species of bats found in Britain, only two have with any certainty been recorded in Orkney, namely, The Pipistrelle or Common Bat, *Pipistrellus pipistrellus* and the Long-eared Bat, *Plecotus auritus*. Though both are comparatively rare, the former is more likely to be encountered and it is probably this species which is referred to by Baikie and Heddle as having been observed in the mid-nineteenth century in St Magnus Cathedral and in an old church in South Walls. Since that time odd specimens have been recorded from time to time, and since the animal appears only at dusk it is probably commoner in Orkney than is generally thought. I can find only two occurrences of the Long-eared Bat, both recorded by the late J. G. Marwick in *The Orcadian*: the first of these was obtained in Sanday in 1931, the second in Holm in 1948.

The Otter, *Lutra lutra*

Otters are abundant both in the Mainland of Orkney and in most of the isles, and have been so from the distant past. More than one hundred years ago, Baikie and Heddle made record of them, adding, 'They feed on fish, which they pursue in freshwater and in the sea. Those of which they appear to be most fond are trout, cod, and conger eels. Having caught a fish and brought it ashore, they commence their meal by devouring the head and shoulders and then usually leave the remainder, which is frequently found lying near their haunts.'

That otters eat birds and mammals as well as fish is perhaps not widely known except by those who have suffered losses among their poultry and farmyard ducks. It is probable that otters take some toll of wild ducks, ducklings, and other sea-fowl as well. In Shetland they have been observed taking Mergansers and Black Guillemots. Their taste seems, indeed, to be quite catholic since they also eat shellfish, crustacea, rats, and mice, and are not infrequently found drowned in lobster-pots.

A full-sized otter may attain a length of four feet and a weight of between twenty and twenty-five pounds. There are two coats of fur; a fine, soft under-coat which is waterproof, and on the outside longer, thicker hairs which give the animal a rather bedraggled appearance when wet. The ears and nose close automatically when under water. The feet, each with five short, pointed claws, are completely webbed. The colour is dark brown, but the otters of Orkney and Shetland are said to be darker than those in the rest of Britain.

Otters are notable for their playfulness in the wild state as well as in captivity, and make attractive and lovable pets. Not so long ago a pair of cubs caught in Graemsay were successfully reared in captivity: one of these, trained by Mr J. Skinner in Stromness, followed him along the street like a dog and was found to be gentle and affectionate. The other, reared in Graemsay, though given complete freedom, always returned from its nightly hunting forays to its household retreat beside the fire.

The Rabbit, *Oryctolagus cuniculus*

Until myxomatosis was brought to Orkney in the early 1950s rabbits were common in the Mainland and the isles, being so numerous in some places as to constitute a nuisance to farmers.

This virus disease spread with dramatic virulence through our rabbit population and led to almost complete extermination in some of the well-known warrens. Places like the Links of Birsay, Burray, and South Ronaldsay became at first a scene of mute suffering where blind lethargic victims stumbled helplessly among the sand dunes, then a graveyard and finally (even as they still are) desolate, cheerless stretches of sand and grass without movement or the familiar bob of white scuts. It was in heavily populated areas that the disease worked its main havoc: more isolated groups or pairs probably survived. During the past three or four years rabbits have become more plentiful again though they are generally encountered only singly or in very small groups: the larger warrens are still deserted; this is the case at least on the Mainland. Rabbit control is undoubtedly a problem for the agriculturalist, and since a healthy doe produces on an average eight young per season, rabbits can increase rapidly. It would be a pity from the naturalist's point of view, however, if this attractive animal were to be totally extinguished. Though the normal colour is greyish brown, numerous reports have reached the writer in the past few years of the incidence in some parts of the county, especially in the Birsay, Harray, and Rendall areas, of rabbits of a ginger colour; this is probably not altogether new, but it appears to be a mutational occurrence of increasing frequency.

The Brown Hare, *Lepus europaeus*

Two kinds of hares are found in Orkney, the Brown Hare and the Blue Hare. Of these, the latter is confined to Hoy, while the former is abundant in the Mainland.

Like rabbits, hares can be a nuisance to the farmer. In the past few years they have increased prodigiously in the Mainland of Orkney so that it is not uncommon in hare shoots organised by the farming community to take toll of more than a hundred hares in a fairly restricted area.

The Blue Hare, *Lepus timidus*

This animal, also called the Scottish, the Alpine, the Variable Hare and in older books, the White Hare, was probably indigenous in Orkney before the Brown Hare. Buckley and Harvie-Brown quote the evidence of the early sixteenth-century traveller, Jo Ben, that 'White hares are there (that is in Hoy) and are caught by dogs'.

It would appear that this species is not found elsewhere in Orkney. It is distinguishable from the Brown Hare by its shorter ears and tail and by its smaller size. The summer coat is greyer than in the case of the Brown Hare, while in winter from early December (but depending to some extent on the weather) this species in Hoy becomes almost completely white, so that when there is no snow on the ground it can be readily detected at a distance and, because of its unusual tameness in winter, can be easily approached within gunshot. Usually, however, they are not shot by farmers since they do not attack crops and have little food value. The average weight of the animal in Hoy is four to five pounds.

The Orkney Vole, *Microtus orcadensis*

The Orkney Vole has the distinction of being the only wild animal peculiar to Orkney. According to one theory it is one of only two surviving variants, the Guernsey Vole being the other, of an otherwise extinct species which lived in Britain at the time when Orkney and Guernsey were still joined to the main mass of Britain and Europe. In other parts of Britain it has been displaced by a later species which still survives in parts of Scotland and the Western Isles, and then by a third species which is found in southern Scotland and England.

On different Orkney islands the Orkney Vole has evolved with slightly varying characteristics. There are, in fact, five sub-species of the Orkney Vole, distinguished from each other by small differences in the details of skull and teeth, while two are separable from the others by the coat colour. The Mainland vole is dark brown in colour, as are those in South Ronaldsay and Burray, whereas those from Westray and Sanday are distinctly lighter. The two last-mentioned are believed to have been cut off from the rest of the stock at an earlier period than the others, the sea depths between these islands and the Mainland being greater than the depths separating the others. So far as I am aware, the Orkney Vole was first mentioned by Barry, minister of Shapinsay, in 1800. It is often found in marshy ground that is covered with moss and short heath in which it makes roads, tracks, or runs of about three inches in breadth and sometimes miles in length, much worn by continual treading and warped into a thousand different directions. Its principal enemy as may be well observed in Orkney, is the Short-eared Owl which may account for as many as two thousand individually in a year. Subsequently to Barry's time the vole appears to have been known to many naturalists, none of whom examined it critically until the end of the nineteenth century when the naturalist Millais made a detailed study of its characteristics and habits.

An interesting feature of the Orkney Vole, at least on the Mainland, is that in some districts many Black Voles are found. The writer has received specimens of these from Rendall, Evie, and Stenness. White Voles are sometimes met with, but they are not so numerous as the black variety. Other colours may be encountered such as a 'rich dark golden russet, verging on red' as reported by the late J. G. Marwick in *The Orcadian* in March 1938. Grey Voles have also been reported in that naturalist's *Notes*.

The Long-tailed Field Mouse, *Apodemus sylvaticus*

The Long-tailed Field Mouse is one of the commonest of British rodents. At least four sub-species have been determined in the British Isles, one of these being in Shetland, one in the Hebrides, and a third in St Kilda. I have no evidence that the Orkney form has been closely studied, and this might be an interesting line of research for some keen biologist. The animal is widespread throughout the Mainland of Orkney and undoubtedly also in the isles, since it is recorded from outlying North Ronaldsay as well as from Shapinsay and other islands.

The colour of the Orkney Field Mouse is normally dark brown but, as in other rodents, there are numerous colour-variations. I have seen specimens which were fairly light grey, with yellowish and brownish hairs interspersed. The underparts are normally white, and the eyes have a prominent, sparkling blackness. Its body is about three and a half inches long with a tail of equal length.

The House Mouse, *Mus musculus*

This timid and inoffensive little creature is too well known to require much description. The length of head and body is between three and four inches, the sparsely-haired, scale-ringed tail being about the same. The fur has a softer, sleeker look than that of the Field Mouse, and the normal colour is a dark, drab brownish grey which is only very slightly paler on the underparts.

The Black Rat, *Rattus rattus*

The Black Rat, originating in the East, became indigenous in Britain in the Middle Ages, and until the introduction in the early eighteenth century of the Brown or Norway Rat, was the common rat of this country. The Brown Rat has steadily supplanted the Black Rat and even in Orkney as early as the second half of the eighteenth century, we find Low recording this fact. By 1848, Baikie and Heddle reported that 'the Black Rat which was said formerly to have been numerous throughout Orkney, is now confined to a single island, South Ronaldsay, and even there is quickly decreasing'.

In the present century, evidence of the continuing existence of the Black Rat has been provided by the following records noted by J. G. Marwick. In September 1932, a Black Rat was received by him from South Ronaldsay—'bluish-black above, ashy-coloured below, with flesh-coloured legs and feet'. In September 1934 another of the same species came from South Ronaldsay, and a third in January 1938. Since that time there are two even more interesting occurrences quoted by the same writer, both in Kirkwall, one in 1940 and a second ('caught in a Kirkwall house') in 1946. It should be added that during the Second World War the Black Rat appears to have been introduced into Westray and is now fairly common there.

The Black Rat is smaller and more slender than the Brown Rat. It has a long pointed snout projecting beyond the lower jaw; the whiskers are long and black—the typical colour is as indicated in the South Ronaldsay specimen quoted above—the ears are long, thin, and naked, and the feet are pink.

The Brown Rat, *Rattus norvegicus*

Since it became established in Orkney a little over two hundred years ago the Brown Rat has steadily supplanted its older cousin. Its destructive habits and repulsive ways make it by far the most obnoxious of our mammals, but there is little doubt that its systematic destruction during the past generation or two, and the more careful disposal of offal and other rubbish, has reduced its numbers considerably, though it is still widespread throughout the Mainland and in some of the isles, and in most parts of our islands the chasing of rats is still one of the attendant excitements of taking in stacks. By tradition they were once numerous in Rousay but mysteriously disappeared from the island about 1836: Buckley and Harvie-Brown state that 'Captain Balfour said he saw the rats leave Rousay in a body, and take to the sea'. In 1858 rats were said to be extinct in Stronsay and Shapinsay, but by 1868 they had again appeared in Stronsay. The same writers say that rats do not live in North Ronaldsay. A report in 1927 stated that only Westray, North Ronaldsay, and North Pharay were then exempt from the Brown Rat, which had been rapidly spreading during the past half-century.

Freakish colouring in the Brown Rat is at least as prevalent as in other rodent species. Piebald specimens, cream-coloured specimens shading to white on the sides, but with black eyes, and pure albinos are sometimes encountered: as well as melanistic or blackish examples. The body may reach a length of nine inches, with a tail of equal length.

The Brown Rat has been named the most powerful natural enemy that civilised man has had to contend with. It is therefore necessary to keep it well under control.

2. SEA MAMMALS

The Grey Seal, *Halichoerus grypus*

The intensive study of this animal in Orkney during the past few years seems to have been chiefly stimulated by a demand on the part of the Scottish Salmon Fisheries for a reduction in its numbers. This is in striking contrast with the fact that, a generation or two ago, protection was enforced to prevent its extinction in British waters.

The first Grey Seals Protection Act was passed in 1914, providing a close season from 1 October to 15 December. At the time it was assessed that Grey Seal stocks round the British Isles had been reduced by slaughter to as few as 500. An investigation in 1927 indicated a British population of from 4,000 to 5,000. In 1932 another Protection Act was passed increasing the close season from 1 September to 31 December, but granting official permission to cancel in particular areas. A recent estimate by Dr Bennett Rae puts the number at between 22,000 and 25,000. The world population is estimated to be about 50,000, the other main centres being at Newfoundland and the Baltic.

The meagre evidence that exists about the Grey Seal in Orkney in past generations suggests that it was not then numerous. Buckley and Harvie-Brown record that at the end of last century the Grey Seal was not common in the sheltered firths of the North Isles. Even as late as the 1930s we have the record of an Eday man (*Orcadian*, 27.12.34) that 'it is only within the last half-dozen years or so that they (i.e., grey seals) have been seen at the Green Holm and elsewhere'. On the other hand, there is evidence that before the building of the Sule Skerry Lighthouse that island, which is now deserted by the Grey Seal, was at one time a popular haunt.

That there has been a large increase is undoubted, since the most recent estimate published by The Nature Conservancy (1962) is that 3,000 Grey Seal pups are born annually on the ten principal breeding islands in Orkney, these being on various isolated holms in the North Isles and in South Ronaldsay. On the Muckle Green Holm alone, in the Westray Firth, nearly 700 seal pups were counted in 1960.

Unlike the Common Seal, which mates at sea and normally takes its young to the sea within the time-stretch of one tide, the Grey Seal has its fixed breeding places where the young are born and lie ashore for from four to six weeks. The time of arrival at the breeding sites for this purpose is October in Orkney. The pup is fed at two-hourly intervals for the first two or three days and thereafter at larger intervals. The fat content of the cow seal's milk is 52 per cent, compared with 3 or 4 per cent for the dairy cow. This rich feeding enables the pup to build up a layer of blubber which is three inches thick at four weeks old and by the end of the third week the pup has trebled in weight, being by that time about 70 lbs. It has at birth a silky white coat which after a few weeks takes on a bluish sheen and is gradually cast.

The Grey Seal is bigger than the Common Seal, weighing up to 700 lbs. in the case of the bull compared with a maximum of 300 lbs. in the case of the Common Seal. The face of the Grey Seal is less round than in the Common Seal: the colour is, however, no reliable guide to identification since both species may be found with varying shades and spotted patterns of grey, blue, and black. The only reliable distinctions are in size, habit, and in teeth-formation.

The current policy of allowing the killing of 750 Grey Seal pups per year in Orkney, has caused considerable local concern. It is feared that the probable result will be that the surviving Grey Seals, shy intelligent animals, will be driven entirely from our shores.

The Common Seal, *Phoca vitulina*

This seal frequents all our coasts, preferring off-shore sandbanks and low tidal rocks to the more remote and rugged habitat of the Grey Seal. The young are born in June or July and, as has been indicated, they take to the water within a few hours. The first coat of the pup of the Common Seal is shed almost immediately after birth. This species may be seen around our coasts at any time of the year.

As regards comparative size, it may be taken as a rough rule that any seal much over six feet long will be a Grey Seal and any adult five feet or less in length will be a Common Seal. Common Seals are quite numerous round our shores though in recent years they are being much reduced in numbers by seal hunters.

Whales

The following cetaceans have been stranded in Orkney at one time or another: Common Rorqual, Lesser Rorqual, Sei Whale, Cuvier's Whale, Sowerby's Whale, Pilot Whale, Risso's Dolphin, Common Porpoise, White-beaked Dolphin, White-sided Dolphin, and Common Dolphin.

A view of Finstown

Stromness

The Churchill Barriers

Rackwick Bay, Hoy

17

OUR ORKNEY FLORA

ONE of the most valuable studies carried out in Orkney during this century was the precise examination of its vegetation by Colonel Henry Halcro Johnston, who left a matchless collection of plants now in the Herbarium of the Royal Botanic Gardens, Edinburgh. After his death in 1940, his field notebooks, one for almost every island in the county, went to Stromness Museum which also houses the collection of an earlier botanist, Magnus Spence. The latter was the author of a book about the plant life of Orkney, *Flora Orcadensis*, now difficult to obtain and much out of date. However, there are many books which will help us in the study of the wild flowers of our neighbourhood, and some of them are named at the end of this chapter.

Every branch of knowledge, including botany, has its share of technical words. The scientific names, which we may learn to use gradually, tell us much more about plants than English names do. The latter often vary in different districts: or sometimes a common name may refer to a particular plant in one place and to an entirely different plant in another area. Scientific names also help us to understand the system of classification, where each obviously or reasonably different plant of the creation may be called a *species*. Closely allied species are grouped into *genera* and genera into *families*. In this brief examination of the flora of Orkney, only the largest families and a few smaller ones of special interest will be considered.

Flowering Plants

Ranunculaceae (some 14 species in Orkney). This is one of the most primitive families in flowering plants and includes the buttercups, both terrestrial and aquatic, the former with yellow, the latter with white flowers. The Bulbous Buttercup, *Ranunculus bulbosus*, is distinguished from the Creeping Buttercup and the upright Meadow Buttercup by its subterranean, perennial bulb, its reflexed sepals, and its earlier flowering. It is common in sandy links. Other examples are the Lesser Celandine, *Ranunculus ficaria*, and the Marsh Marigold, *Caltha palustris*, the latter not a true buttercup but like one, though more primitive. We

9

do not have Larkspur, Columbine, Anemone, Monkshood or the beautiful Globe Flower, a mountain plant reaching Sutherland and Shetland. A species of Meadow Rue, *Thalictrum minus* subspecies *arenarium*, is our scarcest member of this family, being confined to sandy links such as Melsetter, Deerness, Sanday, and South Ronaldsay. It has no petals.

Nymphaeaceae. The water-lilies, *Nymphaea* and *Nuphar* miss Orkney entirely.

Leguminosae (22 species). This large family is of great importance in agriculture. To it belong peas, beans, lentils, pulses, clovers, lucerne, lupins, and whins. You may be acquainted with several of them already but being a large family, naturally quite a few are not represented here. There is a paucity of clovers, peas, and vetches. No account would be complete without mention of the beautiful blue fields of lupins, the introduced *Lupinus nootkatensis* which is, in the end of June, a glorious and unforgettable feature of our landscape.

Umbelliferae (18 species). All the Orkney members of this family have white flowers. The sepals are minute or absent. The small flowers are in compound, less often simple umbels, umbrella-like clusters with the flower-stalks representing the wires. The leaves are much divided. The species are aromatic due to oil-glands, some having an unpleasant smell. Others are well-known vegetables such as celery, carrots, parsley, and parsnips. A few are deadly poisonous, none more baneful than *Cicuta virosa*, the Water Hemlock which Socrates chose for his swift suicide. Orkney *Umbelliferae* include *Heracleum sphondylium*, Cow Parsnip, *Carum carvi*, Caraway, and *Angelica sylvestris*, Wild Angelica. *Ligusticum scoticum*, Lovage, absent in England, occurs on our sea-cliffs, while *Apium inundatum* (no common name) is an aquatic resembling a water buttercup when not in flower.

Myricaceae (1 species). We now come to some woody plants in contrast to herbaceous as this and the next three families will show. *Myrica gale*, the Bog Myrtle or Sweet Gale is one example of the many plants, rare in Orkney but common in other parts of Britain. It looks like a small willow but the leaves have a delightful breeze-borne fragrance. It is native in Eday, the bogs of the Dee of Durkadale, but planted or naturalised elsewhere.

Cupuliferae including Betulaceae, Corylaceae, and Fagaceae (3 species). These are trees and shrubs with catkins including Beech,

Birch, Oak, Alder, Hornbeam, and Hazel. Only Birch and Hazel are native in Orkney, while Alder (not to be confused with Elder) is planted. The Hazel, common in historic times, is dying out. Of the several trees once in Berriedale, only a poor, stunted derelict remains. There was a healthy clump on a rock face at the Kirk Burn, Hoy, but rabbits undermined the rocks and one tree fell into the water and died. The other is still in good condition. It does not produce any nuts but the Berriedale ones did long ago. Nuts are sometimes found in our peat bogs. Visit the 'Wood' at Segal in Hoy to see a pure stand of native Birch.

Salicaceae (12 species). In Orkney the commonest willows are *Salix aurita*, *phylicifolia*, *repens* and *cinerea* subspecies *atrocinerea*, and at least three of their hybrids have been recorded. An interesting dwarf willow, *S. herbacea*, only 2–3 cm. high, occurs on the higher hills. Our rarest willow, a single female clump left now, is *S. myrsinites* form *procumbens*. Even part of that fell down in a landslide from the alpine crags of its precarious habitat. *Populus tremula*, the Aspen, also belongs to this family. No one has ever found its flowers in Orkney, where it spreads by vegetative propagation, suckering freely with the young trees at some distance from the parents.

Ericaceae (11 species). Trees, shrubs and in Britain mostly dwarf shrubs. Some species in this family and the next are very local, being confined to quite small areas of Britain. The same statement applies to Orkney. Such a plant is *Loiseleuria procumbens*, an alpine related to *Rhododendron* and limited to the tops of Hoy's highest hills. Another, a great attraction to visiting botanists, is *Arctous alpinus*, Alpine Bearberry (Inverness to Shetland, nine counties, Hebrides excluded). It occurs in Hoy in considerable quantity above 1,000 feet. Returning to the commonplace, the ubiquitous heather clothes hill and holm in one vast mantle, a purple joy in summer, a sober black in winter like the approach of lonely night. A curious variety of *Calluna vulgaris*, the Ling or Heather, occurs at Tor Ness near Melsetter, shrouding acres of moorland. This variety is invested with a soft white down and if viewed from a distance appears as if a dust storm had blown over it. The Ling is the commonest species in Orkney but no one here ever uses that name. The others are *Erica cinerea*, Bell-Heather, and *Erica tetralix*, Cross-leaved Heath. All three may have white as well as purple or pink flowers and such variants are neither separate species nor varieties.

Pyrolaceae (2 species). This small family is distinguished from the preceding with which it is often united chiefly because its members are herbaceous. It is especially mentioned here because, in the summer of 1963, a party of botanists led by Dr F. H. Perring, made a most unexpected discovery. This was the rare *Orthilia secunda* (formerly *Pyrola secunda*), one of the wintergreens. We have one other, *Pyrola rotundifolia*, which is also rare and local. It occurs in Hoy, Rousay, Orphir, and perhaps elsewhere.

Primulaceae (9 species). A well-known family in horticulture. To it belongs the famous *Primula scotica*, a much advertised attraction for visitors. Many Orcadians are sincerely proud of this little gem, endemic in Orkney, Caithness, and Sutherland. Like a few other rare plants it grows on grassy sea-cliff tops and though recorded from nineteen stations, is far from common in any of them. The public is well-warned not to cultivate it for it never survives long under artificial conditions, even if removed intact with the original turf in which it grew. Watering probably alters its pH requirements, also washing out necessary trace elements from the clod which will not be large enough to retain its original physical properties indefinitely. Another rare plant in this family is *Trientalis europaea*, the Chickweed Wintergreen from Firth and Rendall, while Wood Loosestrife, Bog Pimpernel, and Cowslip are a delight to any nature lover.

Compositae (90 species). This is not only the largest plant family in Orkney but in the British Isles and Europe as well. It contains examples of almost every ecological type and life-form, trees, shrubs, perennial and annual herbs, aquatics, alpine and desert plants, climbers, succulents and spiny shrubs. The small flowers (florets) are aggregated into heads, simulating a single large flower and surrounded by a calyx-like involucre of one or more rows of bracts. The real calyx (pappus) is small, consisting of numerous hairs or small scales which often enlarge when the one-seeded fruit is ripe to act like a parachute, aiding wind dispersal of the fruits. Well known in horticulture are asters, chrysanthemums, marigolds, and double daisies, while others are of economic importance, yielding drugs, oils, perfumes, insecticides, and chicory. The largest genus is *Hieracium*, Hawkweed, a very difficult one, Orkney having twelve species and several varieties. *Taraxacum*, the Dandelion, is even more critical with numerous species differing little from each other, Orkney having some thirty. The humble Coltsfoot, *Tussilago farfara*, one of our earliest spring flowers, is a glad sight in the last dreary days of February, a promise of sunshine, a new spring born again. The leaves appear long after the flower has gone. They were once smoked as a cure for asthma. They resemble those of Butterbur,

Petasites hybridus, from Birsay and Evie, but are smaller. *Solidago virgaurea*, the Golden-rod and *Saussurea alpina*, Alpine Saussurea are mountain plants. The latter with thistle-like, purple flowers seems to be increasing. It grows on the 'hammars' and screes of the Hoy hills and descends to sea-level in Caithness. Changes take place over the years. The lovely Corn Marigold is becoming very scarce today while the blue Cornflower must be hard, indeed, to find. Whole fields of marigold aglow in gold, alternating with verdant rows of turnips adorned the summer. Now the entire picture is green. Other invaders with greater vigour have come to take the place of the ousted. *Matricaria discoidea*, the Rayless Mayweed, was virtually unknown until about 1926. It arrived with poultry food and must now be in every island, far and near.

Orchidaceae (21 species). One of the largest families of flowering plants in the world with 800 genera and 30,000 species, not counting the numerous hybrids of cultivation. The orchid flower in certain species is often weird and fantastic, simulating the shape and colour of animals and insects. As a result some very aptly chosen common names are in use such as Man Orchid, Lady Orchid, Soldier, Monkey, Spider, Fly, Butterfly, Bee, Lizard, Frog, and Bird's-nest Orchids, and many more outside Britain. The absence in Orkney of pine and beech forest, limestone outcrops and chalk downs means the absence of many English species which are restricted to such habitats. We have several of the difficult Marsh Orchids, the *Dactylorchid* group. In Orkney they are best known as *Adam* and *Eve*, the former dark purple and the latter pale lilac. One of our rarest plants is an orchid, *Hammarbya paludosa*, the Bog Orchid, found in sphagnum bogs at Lyra Burn in Hoy.

Cyperaceae (41 species). Cotton-Grass, Rushes, and Sedges (*Carex*). Grass-like plants differing from true grasses in having a triangular stem and a different arrangement of the individual flowers. Orkney has some twenty-seven species of *Carex*, this number being about one third of the total found in the British Isles.

Gramineae (58 species). The grasses with some 600 genera and 8,000–10,000 species are world-wide. The beginner will find both these and the sedges rather difficult and will require to use a hand-lens and a pair of dissecting needles to examine the flower. Cock's-foot, Fescue, Rough and Smooth-stalked Meadow-grass, Rye-grass, Yorkshire Fog, and Brome are well known in agriculture. The rarest grass in Orkney is *Poa alpina*, Alpine Meadow Grass from Hoy.

Cryptogams

These are the *Flowerless Plants* which reproduce by other methods. Their sexual method was for a long time hidden or unknown to botanists. Hence the name *Cryptogams*; their asexual method by spores is readily observable. There are *Vascular* and *Non-Vascular Cryptogams*. The former have vessels in their organs for the conduction of fluids, while the latter do not. To the Vascular Cryptogams belong ferns and fern allies, the allies include Horsetails, Clubmosses, *Selaginella* and Quill-worts. Orkney's rarest fern is the Holly Fern, *Polystichum lonchitis*. Non-Vascular Cryptogams are the Bryophyta (mosses and liverworts), the algae, fungi, lichens, and even bacteria. Fungi, lichens and fresh water and soil algae are imperfectly known as far as Orkney is concerned so only mosses and marine algae will be dealt with here.

Bryophytes (Mosses and Liverworts). Hoy offers the best collecting ground with the rarest species. Like the flowering plants, many mosses and hepatics are lacking in Orkney because of the general absence of chalk, limestone, and wooded areas. Also the paucity of 'Atlantic species', frequent on the damp western coast of Ireland and Scotland, including Sutherland, is a notable feature. Hoy has one or two of them such as the liverworts *Herberta hutchinsiae* and *Anastrepta orcadensis*. The common genera present in the British Isles are also well represented here. *Grimmia maritima* is a maritime moss of rocky seashores just above high-water mark. It fruits in winter during the Christmas holidays. Some species like *Ulota crispa* and *phyllantha* occur on the bark of trees, others like *Fontinalis antipyretica* are found in running water while *Cinclidotus fontinaloides* prefers stones at the edges of lochs. There are alpine mosses, too. One called *Andreaea rothii* may be seen as a black speck on rocks at the tops of the higher hills. *Rhacomitrium lanuginosum* forms stretches of dreary moor in certain parts of Hoy where nothing else, not even heather can grow.

Marine Algae (Seaweeds. About 350 species). There is a wonderful opportunity in Orkney to observe seaweeds for here they occur in unsurpassed luxuriance, unpolluted by the sewage of great towns, washed in all the purity of the northern ocean. The lure of the shore, the call of the sea, the exploration of the unexpected cave round the next headland, the thrill and danger of reaching the wreck, possible only during a March stream, are irresistible attractions to many an Orcadian. There is no end of adventure in the realms of this fascinating group, the marine plants. *British Seaweeds*, 1963, in the Kew series by C. I. Dickinson, is the beginner's book and with it you will find it easy to identify many of the larger or macroscopic species. For the smaller or microscopic ones you will have some difficulties and will require a microscope, just as you will for mosses. This makes your hobby all the more interesting and not something to dread. For purposes of classification seaweeds are usually divided into the Greens, the Browns, the Reds and a fourth, the Blue-greens. These groups occur on the shores in more or less distinct zones and not just anyhow. The Blue-greens occupy the uppermost one and in some cases are above high-water mark, moistened by spray in a splash zone, the Greens come next, stretching from high-water to half-tide, the Browns in a middle one and the Reds from low-water down into what is known as the sublittoral. Examples of Green Algae are *Ulva lactuca* and *Monostroma grevillei*, both known as Sea Lettuce, and *Enteromorpha intestinalis*, a cosmopolitan species with long, inflated filaments like intestines. Kelps, Tangles, Bladder Wracks and Sea Bootlaces are Browns, while *Chondrus crispus*, the Irish Moss or Carragheen, is a Red. We have some rare Reds, several of them southern forms which have found their way here owing to the warm influence of the Gulf Stream in winter. *Fucus distichus*, subspecies *anceps*, a wrack of very exposed rocky coasts, is one of Orkney's specialities. Much has been written about it of late in the *British Phycological Bulletin*.

Summary

The number of species of flowering plants, ferns, and fern allies, including naturalised plants, is, for Orkney, about 653. It is always difficult to give an exact number. The *London Catalogue of British Plants*, 11th edition, 1925, enumerates 2,362 species as the total for the British Isles. Our flora is primarily a north-temperate, herbaceous one with a predominance of heather, grasses and sedges, and the wind-swept bareness and lack of trees at once strikes the newcomer. It would be incorrect to say that there are no trees. There are native species of willow, birch, aspen and rowan and quite a few plantations of sycamores and other non-native trees, but these are often stunted and of smaller stature than in the more sheltered places in the south. The type of soil is an important factor in distribution. We have here no areas of chalk and limestone comparable with the North and South Downs, the Peak District or the Avon Gorge, and no micaceous schists as on the Breadalbanes. Certain plants, many of them rare, are confined to such soils and hence they are absent from Orkney. Others, although not uncommon elsewhere, are rare in Orkney, such as—*Calystegia soldanella*, the Sea Bindweed; *Eupatorium cannabinum*, Hemp Agrimony; *Fragaria vesca*, the Wild Strawberry; *Oxalis acetosella*, Wood

Sorrel; *Rubus chamaemorus*, the Cloudberry; and *Sedum acre*, Wall-pepper. Again the scarcity of woods accounts for the lack of many woodland herbs. Thus Orkney cannot compare with a county such as Surrey in the richness and number of species.

On the other hand, there are a number of northern plants in the county which visitors would wish to see. Some have been mentioned earlier in this chapter, and others are—*Ajuga pyramidalis*, the Pyramid Bugle; *Gentianella amarella*, subspecies *druceana*, a Felwort; *Mertensia maritima*, the Oyster Plant; *Oxyria digyna*, Mountain Sorrel; *Polygonum boreale*, a northern Knot-weed; *Potamogeton filiformis*, Slender-leaved Pondweed; and for specialists, certain species of *Euphrasia* (Eyebrights) and *Hieracium* (Hawkweeds).

Of the five northern areas, east and west Sutherland, Caithness, Orkney, and Shetland, the flora of Orkney is nearest to that of west Sutherland, but it is not so rich: island floras are usually poorer than those of a greater adjoining land mass. Shetland, with a poorer flora than Orkney, has botanically more in common with west Sutherland, as most of its limestone plants are the same as those of Sutherland. Finally, the flora of Caithness is akin to that of east Sutherland, though Orkney and Caithness do have many weeds of cultivation in common.

In the last thirty years there have been a number of significant changes in our flora. From time to time several hitherto unrecorded native plants have been added, the majority in the summer of 1963, and some before that. Other plants have spread to new areas and unfortunately a few are dying or have died out in their localities. Comparatively rare plants, like our favourite *Primula scotica*, are always in some danger, but increasing knowledge and appreciation form the best safeguard of the wonderful and varied flora which we of this age hold in trust.

REFERENCES

Magnus Spence, *Flora Orcadensis*. Kirkwall, 1914.
Clapham, Tutin, and Warburg, *Flora of the British Isles*. Cambridge U.P., 1962.
Edward Step, *Wayside and Woodland Blossoms*. Various editions.
Perring and Walters, *Atlas of the British Flora*. Nelson, 1962.

18

SOME SEASHORE ANIMALS

ONE of the pleasantest ways of spending a sunny afternoon is to explore the contents of rock pools left by the ebbing tide, to search for animals under stones and seaweed, and to see what can be found, in contrast, in the sand of places like the Bay of Skaill, Scapa, or the Bay of Backaskaill in Sanday.

To the person with patience and a careful eye, the seashore teems with animals and plants having all kinds of interesting features. Do you ever see seapinks away from the seashore? Have lobsters been found naturally above high-water mark? Would you see live limpets on sand? The answer in each case is *no*! Every animal and plant has its own range of places where it can live, and this is a very useful idea to keep in your mind when looking for, and at, the living things on the seashore. If you look at the brown seaweeds on a typical rocky shore at low tide, you will find the highest part has a rather ragged-looking weed without bladders, and the fronds curled to form channels. Then there is the common bladder-wrack, followed by serrated wrack, which has toothed edges to the fronds, but no air bladders. At and below low-water mark the tangles start, and go out into fairly deep water. Just as these, and many other, weeds have certain levels on the beach, so, too, do many of the animals. There are several types of barnacles and of whelks which can be distinguished as you go down the shore, but unfortunately they require a certain amount of experience to sort out.

However, let us leave the fine details to the professional zoologists, and see what we can find out in a few trips to the animals of the seashore.

Sea Anemones and Jellyfishes

When visiting a pool left as the tide ebbs, you will notice, stuck on the rocks in the pool, blobs of brown or purple jelly, and objects that look like flowers in bloom. Both are in fact the same animal—no, they are not flowers!—and are some of the zoologist's most interesting animals. There is a great variety of these creatures, ranging from small, not very noticeable ones, to some really big ones which live usually in deeper water offshore. To give them all their proper zoological names is very difficult, but the common ones often have little spots of bright colour around their rims. These are called the 'beadlet' anemones, the spots resembling beads in a necklace.

Now, you will ask, why are some like blobs of jelly while others are like flowers? The flower-like ones are open for feeding. When not feeding, and especially when disturbed, they close up by folding in their feeding 'petals', and then are more resistant to attack or damage. The 'petals' are the feeding arms or tentacles which catch the food, usually small animals and fish in the surrounding water. Each arm carries a large number of stinging structures which shoot a barb carrying poison into the prey when it touches the tentacles, and in this way is quickly paralysed and also held. Then the anemone bends the tentacles over until it pushes its food into the mouth in the middle of the ring of tentacles.

Although the anemone looks immobile, this is not the case. They creep along very slowly on the sticky plate by which they hold on to the rock.

Other common members of this group grow on seaweeds, especially the fronds and stems of tang. They differ from the anemones in being not single animals, but groups of individuals linked by a branching stem that looks even more plant-like than the anemones. The individuals are all small and you will need a powerful magnifying glass to see the details. Instead of each member living for itself, all live for the common good of the colony. Food caught by the feeding members is shared amongst all the little animals. Others do not catch food, but produce what look like tiny jellyfish. These swim off, and later produce the eggs which will found a new colony.

The big jellyfish we see cast up on the shore correspond zoologically to the tiny ones given off by the previous animal living on the kelp. Again, the jellyfish are carnivorous, catching small fish by their stinging tentacles, and drawing them up into the mouth. Sometimes bathers get stung by them, but these are usually windblown stragglers from warm waters, where some are dangerous for swimmers.

It is worthwhile watching for these strange creatures of the sea. And Orkney has plenty of them!

Shellfish or Molluscs

On any shore in Orkney there is a great abundance of shellfish, including mussels, limpets, buckies, whelks, spoots, and cockles. These animals, the molluscs, are unusual in their internal structure, but almost all have a hard shell, or pair of shells, covering their soft bodies. These shells must not be confused with the hard covering of crabs and lobsters and their relatives.

Many of the molluscs can be eaten, and to me there is little more pleasant in taste than a spoot (razor shell) freshly caught on a cold spring evening when the tide is at its lowest ebb. Nowadays, many of these tasty morsels have been forgotten but it is not so long since Orcadians ate a lot more whelks, limpets, cockles, and spoots. I remember a gang of us as boys going whelk-gathering in Sanday, bringing home a bucketful, and boiling them. Then began the exacting job of picking the beast out of its shell with a pin. There seemed so little in each shell, but in a quarter of an hour most of us were full, and there was plenty of empty shells to use as whistles! Limpets lost favour as food earlier than the whelks. But cockles are still eaten quite frequently, probably because they are easier to get and there is more meat in each shell. Spoots were the delicacy, and I wonder how much of this was because they could be caught only at two periods in the year, in spring and autumn when the tides were really low. The method of catching them, too, was fun, as we all walked backwards over the sand, watching for the tell-tale squirt of water which showed the animal had felt our weight on the sand, and had tried to frighten off whatever was there by shooting up a spray of water before burrowing deep into the sand. To catch the spoot, you had quickly to put a knife or a piece of wood into the sand to wedge the razorfish in its burrow before it had time to go deep. Then came the exciting part, scraping away the sand and gently pulling the spoot from its burrow without losing the 'fruit', the fleshy 'foot' of the animal. As the tide flowed, we all went our various ways home, to enjoy our catch fried in butter. Happy days!

But there is more to the apparently simple life of the molluscs than meets the eye. They seem to stay in much the same spot all their lives, and you probably never notice them feeding or doing anything else actively. But the limpet is not the simple thing it appears to be. Most have homes, little depressions in the rock on which they live, from which they move at high tide and at night, to feed by scraping the tiny plant organisms off the surrounding rock. When finished they normally come back to the same resting place. The whelks have the same type of feeding habits in most cases, but the dogwhelks are flesh eaters, boring into other shellfish. Gather a few handfuls of empty buckies next time you are at the shore, and you will find some with neat little holes drilled by the carnivorous dogwhelks.

While the whelks feed on reasonably obvious food, the mussels and cockles are very different. They are known as filter feeders. They sieve from the water millions of tiny living organisms and bits of dead material too small to be seen with the naked eye. To do this, they pump water through their shells, and a complicated system of sticky surfaces catches the food. This is then carried along a system of channels into the mouth.

To see this for yourself, put a few mussels in a big jar of clean seawater, and leave them undisturbed for a while. Then very carefully put a little ink just above the wide back end of the shell, where, if the animals are feeding, you will see two oval, frilly openings. With careful experiment, you will see the ink drawn into the lower opening or being dispersed by the outgoing current from the opening nearer the top humped part of the shell.

The filter-feeding mussel lives exposed on rocks and the cockle burrows in sand. There are many others living in a similar way to the cockle, in sand, and many in mud. Most of the pale or white mussel-like shells you find are from these sandburrowers in deeper waters. The common 'cowfish', with its big brown shells, lives closer inshore, and I have often found it when after cockles.

Lobsters, Partans, Sholties, and Slaters

While the molluscs, or shellfish, are rather stay-at-home, not so the other shelled animals of Orkney. Who hasn't plenty of respect for a live lobster or partan? Almost all the members of this group, the crustaceans, are active swimmers or walkers, and some have come on land. The woodlouse, or 'slater-worm', is a land-invading relative of the lobster or sholtie.

All the common crustaceans are recognised by their many-jointed bodies and rather similar appearance. They are rather like insects, to which they are closely related. Let us look into the secret life of the lobster.

They hatch from the black eggs, or 'berries', carried by the female under her incurled tail in autumn. As babies they float on the surface, too small to be noticed. Soon they sink to the bottom to grow into the familiar lobster. But the shell is very hard, and does not grow. It is like armour on a knight of old. So how does the soft flesh inside the shell find room to grow? Like a knight changing his armour, the lobster throws off its shell periodically, but instead of having a new armour made it simply hardens its skin again, a size larger. While it is doing this, it is helpless and soft, and hides in a dark corner until it is fit to venture out again in a hard case.

Most crabs, sholties, and slaters do the same thing, but the hermit crab has found an easier answer. It tucks its soft tail into an empty buckie, and uses that as armour. When it grows too big for its house, it searches for a bigger one, and quickly flips its tail out of one into the other.

Starfishes and Sea-urchins

The sea animals most likely to puzzle the young naturalist are the sea-urchins and starfishes. Although common, they are not seen as much as they might, as they live at or below low-water mark. Starfishes are usually easy to find at low-tide among rocks, but sea-urchins are usually seen on creels hauled from deeper water.

The starfish's name comes from its shape, often a five-pointed star. But there are some with many more arms. The sea-urchin get its name probably from its resemblance to the unkept head of hair on a human urchin, or street-child. The local Orcadian name, Scarriman's heid, reflects something of the same idea. The 'hair' of the sea-urchin, though, consists of very many hard spines, which protect the animal against enemies. The spines are arranged in bands running up and down the sides of the hard shell. Between the bands of spines you will see equally precise bands of soft, flexible, whitish structures known as the tube-feet. They are hollow and water-filled, and act as hydraulic organs causing movement. Around the mouth some of the tube-feet form special types for feeding. The mouth is on the underside of the animal, and can be recognised by the five pointed teeth projecting from it. If you cut open the shell of a dead urchin you will find a delicate and intricate system of hard supports guiding the teeth. This beautiful structure resembles an old-fashioned lamp and is called Aristotle's lantern.

The lantern is absent in starfishes, but the arrangement of the other parts of the body is very similar. Each arm has tube-feet running down the middle of its under surface and on each side of them are the spines. If you were to fold up the arms of the starfish so that they all met above the animal, you would end up with an animal that resembled a sea-urchin in appearance on the outside. This helps to show how closely alike the two groups of animals really are.

If you find it difficult to see the arrangement of the spines and tube-feet on a living urchin, you will have no difficulty if you find a dead, clean shell. On this, the spines are all lost, as they are attached only by soft material which quickly rots away. But where each spine was attached, there is a little socket. These sockets can now be seen to be in definite rows. In between these rows are lines of tiny holes. In life, the tube-feet came out through these holes from the connecting system inside the animal.

Starfishes and sea-urchins live in the sea, but what do they eat? They differ strongly. The starfish is a flesh feeder, living largely on mussels. But the mussel is not an easy animal to pry from its shell. We can do it only by breaking the shell, or forcing it open with a knife. The starfish has no tools and must rely on its own body. This is where the unusual properties of the tube-feet come into play. The starfish wraps itself around the shell it is opening, attaches its tube-feet and puts on traction between the halves of the shell. Because of the unique hydraulic system driving these tube-feet, it can keep up this force for a long time. The force is not enough to open the mussel straight away, but over the time involved the muscles holding the valves of the mussel shell together get tired and gradually the shell opens. Once there is enough room, the starfish turns its stomach inside out and digests the flesh in the mussel. You could see this for yourself by keeping a reasonably big starfish in a big glass jar of clean, fresh sea-water, giving it mussels as food.

The sea-urchin, on the other hand, is a vegetarian, browsing on tiny plants growing as a green slimy covering on rocks. It wends its way along, scraping off the food as it goes.

Both starfishes and sea-urchins breed by releasing eggs into the surrounding sea-water. The tiny animals which hatch from these eggs look very unlike their parents at first, and float on the surface. But gradually they change to the typical appearance, sink to the bottom and grow into the familiar animals we see cast up after a storm. Keep an eye open for the adults. They are worth a closer look.

REFERENCES

C. M. Yonge, *The Sea Shore*. Collins' New Naturalist Series.
Maurice Burton, *The Margins of the Seas*. Frederick Muller.
Philip Street, *Between the Tides*. University of London Press.

19

WHALES AND SEALS—THE MARINE MAMMALS

EVERY few years or so the newspapers report a stranding of large whales on some sandy bay or other around Britain, very often in Orkney. Usually this is the only time we really take notice of these big animals, which live in deep waters some long way off-shore. Very occasionally we find a single carcase of an animal which has either died or been killed by ships' propellers. However, there is one of the smaller whales which is much more commonly seen around Orkney, and that is the porpoise, a small whale with long, strongly toothed jaws. Its undulating motion through the water is familiar to most of us who enjoy a night at the cuithes.[1] On a good calm night it is often possible to hear the sough of its breath through its blowhole every time it surfaces for air.

Another denizen of inshore waters is the seal. At first thought it might seem to be very closely related to the whales, but in fact the resemblance is due much more to the fact that they both live in water than to any real relationship. Our common selkie, however, can be taken as an example familiar to us all which will show how all these marine mammals are modified for living in water.

How are we to explain how these mammals took to the water while most of the mammals we know are living on land? The answer lies in the ability of animals to use any source of livelihood and food which is open to them. The sea is a rich foodstore which man has hardly even begun to tap by his fishing methods, and, as the world population grows, he is going to have to rely more and more on the food he can harvest from the sea. But the marine mammals have beaten us to this by returning from the land many millions of years ago, and now being very efficiently adapted for living in water.

What are these adaptations? When we swim, we find it hard work, simply because of our very poor shape for moving in water. And we have no good method of using our bodies to propel us along; we have to rely on our small hands and feet, using muscles which are too weak to produce much useful effort in water. On the other hand, the shape of fishes, seals, and whales is streamlined so that these animals have very

[1] A night's fishing.

little resistance to the flow of water over their bodies. From the start, therefore, the amount of effort required to go through the water is reduced. Add to this the strong tail of fishes and the well-developed flippers and tail of the seals and whales, and we see how much more efficiently such animals are adapted for swimming. When we compare the main swimming organs of fish and marine mammals, we find a very strong similarity between them at first sight, and it is only when we study them more deeply that we see how they have arisen from completely different parts of the animal's bodies. The tail of the fish is a true tail in the zoological sense, but the so-called tail of the seal and whale is really a modification of the back legs of the more typical mammal types. These legs have become turned backwards and flattened to form the large surface used in driving the animal through the water. The similarity in general appearance is due entirely to the requirements of swimming in water.

FIG. 5   (a) The horizontal flukes of a whale's 'tail'.
(b) The vertical tail of a typical fish type.

To support this, compare the direction of motion of the fish's tail with the whale's. In fish the tail is moved from side to side and is flattened from side to side. The flukes of the whale, on the other hand, are flattened from top to bottom (Figure 5), and the flukes are moved up and down to give the driving force in movement. The seal, however, is still not so well adapted for living in water as the whale, and still spends a lot of its life lying on rocks to digest its food, and to give birth to its young and suckle them. The hind flippers of the seal bear out this contention, as they still can be seen to be derived from two obviously foot-like structures. Next time you come across a seal or a small whale cast up dead on the shore look for these features, and see whether you agree.

But if you are looking for the other mammalian feature, hair, you may find it more difficult to agree with me, as the hair of a mammal is not necessarily beneficial to a water-living animal. In the seal, of course, the hair is very strongly developed, giving, as it does in the land animals, an insulation against cold. The air trapped in the meshwork of the hair serves to keep the contact between the cold water and the actual skin of the animal to a minimum, and for this reason it is a good material for

A Kittiwake colony in the cliffs

A regatta in Kirkwall Bay

The 'butt-end' a kitchen of the old Orkney pattern

Sunset over Scapa Flow

making coats for man in very cold climates—think of the Eskimos who use it for this purpose.

But you will remember that I said earlier that the seals are less well adapted for living in water than are the whales. These animals have lost almost all their hair, and rely on a thick layer of fat, or blubber, under the skin to preserve their heat. The seal also has this layer, but not so well developed as in the whales. In fact, about the only hair on a whale is a collection of small bristles on the front of the head. So when you look at your stranded whale, this is where to look.

On mentioning blubber in whales and seals, we must also think back to the times in Orkney before electricity and oil were brought in by modern industries. What did people use for their light in winter nights? You will probably have heard of, and seen, a cruisie lamp. This usually home-made affair was designed to burn the oil from the blubber of seals and whales, using a rush stem as a wick. Also, some of the fats from the blubber were mixed with beeswax and used to make candles, again using either a rush or a piece of twine as a wick. Needless to say, these very simple affairs did not give out much light.

Feeding of Seals and Whales

Since we do not usually see how seals and whales feed, we naturally are curious to find out. There are two main sources of food, and along with them, two methods of feeding. All the local seals are flesh-eaters, living on fish which they catch by chasing. Consequently, we should beware of handling a seal carelessly, as they can give a nasty bite, a big seal being able to remove a hand. Having fed in the sea, most of the seals lie on the surface, or come to bask on the shore to digest their food.

Among the whales, on the other hand, some are flesh-eaters, and some, including the very biggest whales, live on tiny animals which they sieve from the water. Among the flesh-eaters are the porpoises we see around our shores. Again, the prey is fish. And, as in the seals, the jaws are strong and shaped for handling this type of food.

The bigger whales, however, have a fascinating modification for catching the small animals, or 'krill', which they eat. Instead of powerful biting jaws, they have a very large mouth, whose inside is hung with curtain-like screens of material similar to our finger-nails, called 'baleen'. These screens of baleen are frilly, and act as sieves. The whale fills its mouth with sea-water and any krill that may be in the water. It then closes its mouth partially, and expels the water through the frilly baleen. Any krill are trapped and swallowed. In this way, a big whale from deep water will catch and consume up to several tons of krill per day.

The krill themselves are like tiny lobsters, being fairly closely related to the lobster family. They measure about an inch or a little more in length, and weigh only a fraction of an ounce each. They are found in greatest abundance where the cold water from the Arctic meets the warmer waters coming north in the Gulf Stream, and it is here that the whales are caught. The sea around Greenland used to be very rich in such whales, and they were often hunted by our Orcadian forefathers who might spend half of the year off at the 'whaling'. Nowadays, unfortunately, there are rather few of these whales left.

Such large whales are rarely seen in the vicinity of Orkney, and I mention them here because they gave so much employment to Orcadians in earlier days, and because their jawbones can still be seen in various parts of Orkney as gateposts. Also, the individual bones of their spines used to be employed by crofters as bases for stack steethes, in the days when stacks were built up off the ground.

The whales which are commonly seen around our shores are the porpoises. They live on fish, not krill, and for this reason they are not a welcome sight when we go to the cuithes. They tend to make the fish cautious, and people say that it is no good going to the cuithes if porpoises are about. How much truth there is in the saying I do not know, as I have seen porpoises, and still had a reasonable catch of cuithes. What I have noticed, however, is that seals following a cuithe boat will spoil the night's fishing.

The porpoise is of scientific interest in that it is a very efficient swimmer indeed, and modern research in submarines has borrowed some ideas from the porpoise to help reduce the drag of the water on the hull. The porpoise's skin moulds itself to the varying pressure of the water as the porpoise moves along. In this way the drag is reduced. Submarine designers have tried to use foam plastic in the same way, with some success, but they have still to equal the porpoise in efficiency.

You may have also asked yourself how a school of porpoises can keep in formation so well, and how they all surface to breathe at the same time. The answer is that they make squeaky noises under the water, and they can hear and respond to these noises much as we do with speech. It is possible that they also know how far they are from the bottom and from rocks by sending out their squeaks and listening for the echo. They certainly can find food by using this echo-location method. Not only can they locate obstacles by their own squeaks, but it seems that they can hear other sounds under water very well, and it has been suggested that they could be trained to locate enemy submarines by the noise of their engines long before any modern scientific listening devices could do so. Porpoises, of course, are very easily trained to do all sorts of tricks, such as jumping through hoops, and feeding from the hand, so that training them to respond to sounds is not at all difficult. They are also notoriously playful animals, and are well worth watching for this alone.

Problems facing Diving Mammals

One of the most interesting problems one comes across when studying marine mammals is how they are able to stay under water for prolonged periods of time, and how they do not suffer from the 'bends' as do human divers in diving suits. The bends are caused by a build up of nitrogen gas in the blood when the human diver is under increased air pressure to maintain a constant flow of air through his airline from the surface. When he resurfaces, this gas comes out of solution in the blood, and forms bubbles of free nitrogen. These frothy bubbles usually get trapped near joints such as the knee and the elbow, and various other places, and can be very painful indeed, or even lethal.

Whales and seals obviously do not have a constant piped supply of air, but fill their lungs only at the surface. Consequently, they must take down with them all the oxygen they need while they are submerged. However, from a knowledge of the properties of whale blood and other oxygen-storing systems in the muscles it has been calculated that the amount taken down in these stores is nowhere near enough to maintain the work-rate of the animal as measured when it is on the surface. How then does the whale or seal manage to stay down for periods longer than its oxygen supply would appear to last? In some seals this period of submergence is a maximum of about 15 minutes, and in some whales, up to 90 minutes. The answer to the question is very clever. The animals turn off, as it were, the vast bulk of oxygen-using organs in their bodies, and reserve as much as possible of the oxygen for use by the muscles of movement, for the heart to pump the blood, and for the brain, which cannot under any circumstances do without oxygen for more than a few seconds. The muscles themselves can also to a slight extent change over the chemical methods by which they produce energy, and run up a slight debt of oxygen, which is then refunded when the animal surfaces.

As a consequence of this turning off of many organs during the dive, we find that most of the digestion is done when whales are lying on the surface, and when seals are lying on the rocks, or floating and breathing air directly.

The spouting of whales, which the whale catchers of old used as a means of spotting their prey, and which they signalled to their steersman by the call, 'There she blows!', is simply the means by which the whale blows out the stale air in its lungs and takes in fresh air. It does this several times to build up its stores of oxygen before it can dive again for any prolonged period of time. To make it easier for the whale to take in air quickly when it surfaces, there is an interesting modification in that the nostrils, instead of being at the front of the head as in most animals, are moved to the top of the head. Hence, the animal has merely to break the water surface instead of sticking its head well out of the water. You will have noticed that the selkies do not have this modification, as they stick their snouts and a considerable part of their head out of the water when they come up for air.

There is still another modification in the marine mammals to help them in their deep diving. I mentioned earlier the 'bends'. The whales and seals avoid this merely because they do not breathe under water. In this way, the nitrogen in their blood is not increased while they are under the pressure of the water, so that when they come up to the surface there is not any surplus of nitrogen in the blood to form bubbles. But what of the nitrogen that was in the lungs when the animal dived in the first place, you may ask? Another interesting property of the lungs of these animals appears here. Before diving, the animals expel most of the free air in the lungs, so there is no surplus nitrogen or oxygen to be picked up there by the blood. Also when the pressure of the water increases as the animal dives deeper, the lungs collapse under the pressure, and any little residue of air is forced up into the wind-pipe, where it is not absorbed readily. To allow this collapse of the lungs, the material in them is elastic and, when the pressure is reduced on surfacing, they quickly resume their normal shape and size.

Perhaps the scientifically most fascinating adaptation of diving mammals I have kept to the end. This concerns the rate of heart-beat. But first, of all, let us consider the heart of a land mammal such as man himself. Our normal heart-beat is around 72 per minute when we are at rest. Normal variations between various people may run up to 10 beats per minute more or less than this figure. In some people, such as athletes, the heart may be developed in a way that it may go to a much lower figure at rest. Figures as low as 44 to 48 are not abnormal, but are rather unusual. During exercise the rate goes up very quickly to supply the necessary oxygen from the lungs to provide energy for muscle working. Our own hearts can go up to very high rates, of the order of 200 beats per minute. This activity of the heart depends on muscular work, just as does ordinary movement of the body. And since all muscle contraction needs a supply of oxygen to release energy this heart work takes up a substantial amount of oxygen.

It is here that the fascinating adaptation of the seal's heart, and probably that of the whale as well, comes in. As soon as the seal dives, its heart-beat, normally about 150 per minute, drops right down to about 10 per minute. In this way, the seal is conserving a goodly amount of its oxygen supply, and at the same time maintaining just enough blood flow to supply the brain and the muscles. Furthermore, while this drastic cut in the rate of heart-beat might be expected to lead to a sharp drop in the pressure of the blood, in fact such a thing does not happen, because as the pulse slows, the pressure is kept up by small muscles along the blood-vessels causing narrowing of the vessels, and in this way keeping the blood-pressure up to its normal level.

While none of these facts are easy to see without fairly complicated scientific experiment, they do help us to realise just how well these diving mammals are modified to suit their method of life, and this adaptation of animals to their ways of living is one of the most important ways of understanding why an animal can do things which at first sight seem to us, as human beings, to be rather remarkable.

PART TWO

Some Orcadian Writers

ERIC LINKLATER was born in 1899, the son of Captain Robert Linklater, of Dounby, Orkney. A young soldier during the '14–'18 war, he was seriously wounded in France while serving with the Black Watch. Several years of study at Aberdeen University were followed by life in Bombay, as assistant editor of the *Times of India*. He returned to university work in Aberdeen and in the United States, but his inclination was for writing. His first novel, *White Maa's Saga*, published in 1929, gained immediate appreciation, especially in his native Orkney. Since then a stream of novels, essays, and plays has placed him in a foremost position among modern authors. Some of these are: *Poet's Pub* (1929), *Juan in America* (1931), *Magnus Merriman* (1934), *The Man on my Back* (1941), *Private Angelo* (1946), and *The Ultimate Viking* (1955).

His writing was interrupted by service during the Second War, first as commander of the Orkney (Fortress) R.E. (T.A.), and later in the Directorate of Public Relations, War Office. He was Rector of Aberdeen University from 1945 to 1948, and in 1951 he was re-commissioned as Lieutenant-Colonel for a brief mission to Korea.

THE ISLAND OF GAIRSAY

BEYOND the last cliffs of Scotland and the crested surge of the Pentland Firth, in the very midst of the archipelago that Tacitus called the Orcades, lies the island of Gairsay. It consists of a round hill, dark in hue above a broad green forefoot, with a bluff peninsula known as the Hen; and close beside is the attendant islet of Sweyn Holm. South of it, like outposts for its defence, are skerries in a white contest of breaking waves: the Holm of Rendall, Seal Skerry, the Holm of Boray, Taing Skerry, and Grass Holm—and the land-girt but rough waters of Wide Firth, at the southern corner of which the cathedral of St Magnus, rose-tawny under a westering sun, dominates with the negligence of eight hundred years' authority the small, self-satisfied and thriving town of Kirkwall.

The hill of Gairsay is three hundred feet high, and the island measures a little more than a mile from north to south, about the same from east to west. The nearest shore, of the parish of Rendall in the West Mainland of Orkney, is less than a mile distant, but the strait between is swiftly tidal and there is no formal communication across it

In the summer of 1953, when a growing ambition persuaded me to return to the island, which I had not visited for several years, I had to go to Kirkwall in the early morning and take passage with two fisher-men who were setting out to attend their fleet of lobster-creels. We had a voyage of seven or eight miles. . . .

It was a day—when I went ashore—of sun and rain, of cloud and moments of transparent visibility, and the bordering sea was a pel-lucid grey, a rippled glass above grey shingle, on which brown eider-duck with a tail of young swam mildly to and fro, divorced all summer from their gaudy drakes.

It was to look at the stage of its short scene in history that I went to Gairsay, and the birds deserved some attention because they were economically related to history. They too had suffered changes, but the island in its turbulent days may have harboured as many, and as many different sorts, as now in its deserted stillness. A wisp of snipe—a vibration of snipe—rose abruptly from the corner of a reedy pool, and oyster-catchers in their pied livery pretended a shrill excitement. I walked on sheep-cropped grass by a deserted schoolhouse and past a ruined farm. On the flat green parts of the island there were the ragged remains of three or four farmhouses with their byres and stables, and the hill was girdled by a broken drystone wall and an older turf dyke, collapsed and undermined by rabbits: a 'fail dyke' of the sort that made scenery for a ballad:

> In ahint yon auld fail dyke
> I wot there lies a new-slain knight,
> And naebody kens that he lies there
> But his hawk, his hound, and his lady fair.

The fail dyke led to a narrow bay separating the main part of the island from the peninsula called the Hen. Three herons rose slowly on heavy wings as I approached it, and from the middle of its calm water a seal thrust its smooth head and wide inquisitive eyes. At the innermost curve of the bay there was, mysteriously, the severed bow of an old herring-boat, apparently one of the large, swift-sailing, sea-fearless sort known as Zulus. It was here, in Millburn Bay, that Sweyn Asleifson in the 12th century must have hauled and tented his longship when he came home from his autumn cruising and settled down for warm winters of ale and mead, of women's gossip and the bickering of eighty men-at-arms that he kept about him; but there was nothing now to remind one of the last of the great vikings except the barren islet that preserved his name, and the mansion-house built on the foundations of his drinking-hall.

I turned from the shore to climb the hill, and on the fail dyke four molliemawks—fulmars, or St Kilda gulls—watched me with a dark and boreal gaze. Three sat closely round one that was brooding in a cleft of the dyke. Two got up leisurely, the third vomited a white mess to reduce its weight and then, still heavy-laden, flew ponderously down-hill. I lifted the sitting bird and saw an egg held firmly in the feathers of the brooding-patch; and as if it shared a human curiosity a wren flitted over the dyke and perched beside me. The fulmars were new-comers since the days of the vikings. Seafarers and persistent colonists, sailing on resolute and efficient wings towards the south, they were indeed the later Norsemen of the air.

Over the top of the hill, crying noisily, flew a screen of common gulls and herring-gulls, and while I stood to look at a view of hills and islands I heard through the harsh tumult of the sea-mews a thin piping note, and presently perceived a golden plover, elegant in its black bib, con-versing in a strain of gentle melancholy with its mate that stood on a farther ridge. Another pair appeared, and their small voices seemed to join in general conversation.

To the west rose the hills of the Mainland of Orkney, the largest of the islands, and in their changing colours I could read the history of the last hundred years; a history of progressive farming that has carried the green hues of grass and clover, of oat-fields and root crops, square after square, higher and higher up dark slopes of peat and heather. To the east lay the islands of Shapinsay and Stronsay—but the farther-off was soon lost in cloud—and to the north the highland shape of Rousay and a dark glimpse of Eday. In between were lesser islands: low upon the sea the reticent flat lines of Wyre, and Egilsay sprouting the high round tower of a tiny roofless church of the twelfth century: a tower like a great chimney, fifty feet tall and narrowing to a broken summit.

Rousay, its hills surging to the north—the midmost rearing like a wave before some cosmic gale—bore memories far older than vikings. In Rousay were neolithic graves and brochs of the Iron Age, and I remembered vividly my first sight of a great cairn of many chambers on its west shore; for it had made on my mind a singularly cold impression of antiquity. The hidden tale of prehistory was not the object of my search, but I could not ignore it because the story I wanted to tell had to be given a foundation. I had to show that Orkney, under its Norse earls, was of some political importance, and its importance could more easily be accepted, as a natural development, after considering the economy of its first colonisation in the Stone Age.

As I walked downhill, over grass starred with tormentil to a shore where black rocks were parti-coloured with the yellow tangle of the sea, and the sea was still glass-grey, I became aware of an extraordinary physical pleasure. It suffused my body and possessed my mind. Eyes and ears contributed to it, but my lungs were filled with it—I breathed the euphory that blows down from an arctic spring—and I realised that physical exhilaration must be accepted as a factor in Norse history, an impulse in the viking mood; and it helps, indeed, to explain much that the vikings did. If the warmth of the Mediterranean has been fertile of history, so has the polar wind been procreant. . . .

Eric Linklater, *The Ultimate Viking*. Macmillan & Co. Ltd., 1955.

THE LAKE

The lake is subject to the sky, and about these northern islands the sky, from day to day, is a drunken hooligan, a dance of Cupids, a rout of silver-breasted Cuirassiers, a weeping savage, or a temple for the Princess of China. The lake replies. As well as water may, it echoes gaiety and gloom, youth in its morning rage, beauty in her pride or naked in her innocence. It has no constant quality. In winter it will drown its green islets, in summer its banks are hidden by meadowsweet and flags.

It is quick with many birds, with mallard and merganser and the black-headed gull. A tight rabble of coots, rising in sudden alarm, with staccato clapping of their wings will scuttle in a crystal storm from the shelter of a bay. In June comes idly sailing a fleet of swans, and that exquisite warrior, the Arctic tern, hangs like a hawk in the unmoving air. A few pairs of eider-duck prefer its sweet water to the sea, and while a cormorant on a rock holds out heraldic wings to dry, redshanks with indignant whistle patrol the shore.

Three arms of the lake stretch to the north and south and west. The southern arm, which is the longest, divides an antique burial-ground, called Maeshowe, from a circle of standing stones that long ago was raised in honour of the breeding sun, or to gratify the mysterious fertility of the moon. In the beginning the stones may have been alternately male and female symbols: among antiquarians there is stubborn opinion and fierce belief, but no certain knowledge; and I have a mind as open as perfect ignorance can make it. No one knows who drew the circle, or for whom Maeshowe was built with such gigantic labour and mathematical precision. The masonry is heroic in scale, the plan was drawn by a geometer; but it lies between moorland and the lake, in a simple country that has little wealth except the colour of its sky. What queens or gods forgotten were buried in its three chambers, and who were the people that closed their tombs with massive blocks of stone? No one knows. The country is very old, and in these small and distant islands age seems the more remarkable. In Babylon and Crete, in the middle of the world, antiquity is natural, and the oldest human tales are domesticated there. But here in Orkney we are beyond the perimeter of ancient knowledge. Britain itself is barely on the fringe of history—a shadow-story of Palaeolithic men, some finger-prints of the noble Age of Bronze—and from Britain our neighbour-island we are separated by the whirlpools and Atlantic-muscled tide of the Pictland Firth. Yet there are graves and subterranean dwellings that feel as cold as Nineveh. Four thousand years ago, perhaps, men stood where I live now, and in the evening-mirror of the lake—a thunder-blue reflexion—saw the round hills of Hoy.

The western arm of the lake goes bluntly to within a couple of miles of the sea. A line of low hills divides it from the Atlantic, and westward of those hollow cliffs there is no nearer land than Labrador. The shores of the lake are heatherland, green banks, or cultivated fields. Its northern arm is shallow, and good for trout-fishing. A rushy stream enters the farthest bay, and here, about fifty years ago, the trout swam ashore in such numbers that near-by farmers brought down their carts, and with dung-forks loaded them full and counted their catch by the hundredweight.

On a heathery knowe, by the northern arm of the lake, my father built a house; and when I was eleven or twelve years old he bought me a boat. The lake and the boat became my partners in a game of doing nothing that lasted for many summers. Day after day I spent, solitary, idle as a dog at sea, or fishing with a mind intent only on the dropping flies and the bubble of a rising trout. My chief talent was for idleness, and to lie in a drifting boat was a pleasure that did not grow stale. There was the wrinkled water to look at, the sky in lofty vacancy or wild with smoking cloud, the merganser with its tail of tiny ducklings. There were the terns that came always in the same week of the year, and always a pair of them sat on the same flat rock at Grutness, resting after their flight from Africa. There were the hills with the old names—Hindera Fiold and Syradale and the Kame of Corrigall—and beyond them a thought of the lesser islands with their sprawling shape and circling tides. . . .

SCAPA FLOW

There is, indeed, a power in the land, or in the broad sky enclosing it, that may take perpetual captive those who are rash enough to open their eyes to the endlessly flowing line of its hills, their ears to the curlew's cry and the burdoun of the sea, their hearts to the northern peace. On a fine morning, when the winds are still and the lakes relume an azure sweep of sky, vacant but for a curd of cloud, a mallard and its mate, there is a hush like the drifting of the young earth, not wakened yet, in the innocence of time. There looks to be no movement on the land but smoke rising slowly from a cottage hearth, the peewits dancing, the deliberate pace of a ploughman and the horse straining stiffly against its collar. There is silence, as it seems, without note or cry to break it, till you too fall silent and catch with livelier ears the small bright talk of linnets in the heather, the creaking fall of a lapwing, the tentative voice of a plover, or the thresh of a rising swan, and far away the Atlantic rolling its organ-tongue in a cavern of the western cliffs.

*   *   *

In such weather, in a boat that soared lazily and softly fell upon the sleeping pulse of the Atlantic, I have lain below the great cliffs of Hoy, that rise eleven hundred feet sheer above the sea. In the evening light they were red as a wine-stain, and flowing from their pillared walls, a tropic air, came the gathered warmth of the day.

Such a day I have spent on Scapa Flow, when the surface of the sea was like polished marble, in the distance reflecting light, but overside impenetrably black. Save the engine-throb, there was no sound but the liquid falling of the bow-wave, a crystal semilune that cut the stillness like a plough, and heaped upon it a sparkling ridge of rough translucent water. On the one side, below a nacreous sky, were the round hills of Hoy, and on the other a coloured shore that stained the reflecting sea with pale red, and yellow corn. Rounding a low point, the boat came into shallow water, a green transparency that showed a bottom of pale sand on which tall seaweed grew. A shoal of little fish fled from the shadow of the boat. A flock of kittiwakes, startled, rose from a stony beach and doubled their number in the mirror of the sea. The stiff and sudden clamour of their wings was clearly audible, and the down-draught of their flight struck the wet beach like a breeze from the hill. A mile away, in a ripe field, a reaper clattered softly through yellow straw. A cormorant, with reaching neck and sluggish wings, flew past us with a jarring noise.

We crossed to the island of Hoy, and in a shallow bay anchored on a glittering shore. Here and there, in a submarine dust-storm, a small flounder was put to flight, and presently in the floor of the sea we could discern, like tiny yellow jewels, the eyes of cockles buried in the sand. A seal, with mild inquisitive gaze, swam slowly round. Two or three miles away, on a shoal called the Barrel of Butter, lay a whole rookery of seals, somnolent in the afternoon, and like lean philosophers a few herons pondered in the ebb. The southern isles stood on a ridge of light above the sea, and to the north-east, above the town of Kirkwall, rose the cathedral spire of St Magnus.

This great red church, that was built eight hundred years ago, is the heart of the islands. . . .

Eric Linklater, *The Man on my Back*. Macmillan & Co. Ltd., 1941.

EDWIN MUIR (1887–1959), was born in Deerness, on the Mainland of Orkney. His early years were spent fairly happily in the islands, where his father was a farmer, but, when he was fourteen, the family moved to Glasgow. After a difficult period there, he married Willa Anderson in 1919, and with her went to London, and then for five years to Prague, Germany, Austria, and France. The two achieved distinction by their translations of German books, while Muir became a regular contributor of articles and reviews to various publications. His best known prose work is *The Story and the Fable* (1940), revised and enlarged in *An Autobiography* (1954). From 1950 he was for five years the distinguished warden of Newbattle Abbey College, a centre of adult education, near Edinburgh.

In 1925, he published a book of *First Poems*, and with later books of verse his reputation grew steadily as one of our major poets. *Collected Poems*, published in 1960, edited by Willa Muir and J. C. Hall, is his fitting memorial.

WYRE

THE Orkney I was born into was a place where there was no great distinction between the ordinary and the fabulous; the lives of living men turned into legend. A man I knew once sailed out in a boat to look for a mermaid, and claimed afterwards that he had talked with her. Fantastic feats of strength were commonly reported. Fairies, or 'fairicks' as they were called, were encountered dancing on the sands on moonlight nights. From people's talk they were small, graceful creatures about the size of leprechauns, but pretty, not grotesque. There was no harm in them. All these things have vanished from Orkney in the last fifty years under the pressure of compulsory education.

My father left the Folly for a farm called the Bu in the island of Wyre. There were seven other farms on the island, with names which went back to the viking times: Russness, Onziebist, Helzigartha, Caivit, Testaquoy, Habreck, the Haa. The Bu was the biggest farm in the island, and close beside a little green knoll called the Castle. In the eleventh century this had been the stronghold of a viking freebooter called Kolbein Hruga, or Cubby Roo, but we did not know this at the time, nor did any of our neighbours: all that remained was the name and the knoll and a little cairn of big stones. Between the house and the knoll there was a damp green meadow which waved with wild cotton in summer. Then came the dry, smooth slope of the Castle, and on the top the round cairn of square grey stones, as high as a man's shoulder and easy for us to climb. My younger sister and I would sit there for hours in the summer evenings, looking across the sound at the dark, hilly island of Rousay, which also had its castle, a brand-new one like a

polished black-and-white dice, where a retired general lived: our landlord. He was a stylish, very little man with a dapper walk, and the story
went that because of his size he had been the first to pass through the
breach in the wall of Lucknow when that town was relieved during the
Indian Mutiny. He came over to Wyre every spring to shoot the wild
birds. I remember one soft spring day when the light seemed to be
opening up the world after the dark winter; I must have been five at the
time, for it was before I went to school. I was standing at the end of the
house; I think I had just recovered from some illness, and everything
looked clean and new. The General was walking through the field
below our house in his little brown jacket with the brown leather tabs
on the shoulders, his neat little knickerbockers and elegant little
brown boots; a feather curled on his hat, and his little pointed beard
seemed to curl too. Now and then he raised his silver gun, the white
smoke curled upward, birds fell, suddenly heavy after seeming so
light; our cattle, who were grazing in the field, rushed away in alarm at
the noise, then stopped and looked round in wonder at the strange
little man. It was a mere picture; I did not feel angry with the General
or sorry for the birds; I was entranced with the bright gun, the white
smoke, and particularly with the soft brown tabs of leather on the
shoulders of his jacket. My mother was standing at the end of the house
with me; the General came over and spoke to her, then, calling me to
him, gave me a sixpence. My father appeared from somewhere, but
replied very distantly to the General's affable words. He was a bad landlord, and in a few years drove my father out of the farm by his exactions.

Between our house and the school there was a small, roofless chapel
which had once been the chapel of the Castle. In summer it was a
jungle of nettles and rank weeds, which on hot days gave out a burning
smell that scorched my nostrils. At the school, which stood on a slight
rising, a new group of more distant islands appeared, some of them
brown, some green with light sandy patches. Not a tree anywhere.
There were only two things that rose from these low, rounded islands:
a high, top-heavy castle in Shapinsay, standing by itself with the insane
look of tall, narrow houses in flat, wide landscapes, and in Egilsay a
black chapel with a round, pointed tower, where St Magnus had been
murdered in the twelfth century. It was the most beautiful thing within
sight, and it rose every day against the sky until it seemed to become a
sign in the fable of our lives. . . .

My first definite memories are connected with the Bu; but there is
one composite one which may conceivably go back to the house where
I was born, it brings such a sense of timelessness with it. I was lying
in some room watching a beam of slanting light in which dusty,

bright motes slowly danced and turned, while a low murmuring went on somewhere, possibly the humming of flies. My mother was in the room, but where I do not know; I was merely conscious of her as a vague, environing presence. This picture is clear and yet indefinite, attached to one summer day at the Bu, and at the same time to so many others that it may go back to the day when I first watched a beam of light as I lay in my cradle. The quiet murmuring, the slow, unending dance of the motes, the sense of deep and solid peace, have come back to me since only in dreams. This memory has a different quality from any other memory in my life. It was as if, while I lay watching that beam of light, time had not yet begun.

My first definite memory is of being baptised. Why I was not baptised in Deerness, where there were two churches, I have never been able to find out; but the ceremony was postponed for some reason until I was three years old. I was dressed for the occasion in a scarlet suit with petticoats instead of breeches, for boys were not given boys' clothes then until they were five. The suit was made of some fine but slightly rough material like serge; the sun must have been shining that day, for the cloth seemed to glow from within with its own light; it was fastened with large glittering golden buttons. I think it must have been the first time that I saw the colour of gold and of scarlet, for it is this suit that makes me remember that day, and it still burns in my memory more brightly than anything I have ever seen since. In the afternoon my father and mother led me by the hand to the school, where Mr Pirie, the minister of Rousay, had come to baptise me. Some people had gathered. I was lifted up by my father, face upward; I saw Mr Pirie's kind face with its thin beard inclined diagonally over me (for he had a glass eye and looked at everthing from the side), then I felt the cold water on my face and began to cry. As if the baptismal water had been a deluge, all the rest of that day is damp and drowned, the burning scarlet and the gold sunk in darkness.

Most of my childhood is drowned as deep as the rest of that baptismal day; I have no recollection of the routine of my first seven years, though it was there, giving me my first realisation of order in the world. A fragment of that age swam up recently after being lost for more than sixty years. It was another suit of clothes, and it returned by a curious road. I was down in Edinburgh a few years ago with some time on my hands. I went into a tea-room, and after having my tea looked round to see what the hour was, but there was no sign of a clock. As the waitress was giving me the bill I asked her the time; she glanced at a wrist-watch she was wearing, and told me with a condescending air that it was a quarter to six. As I still had some time left I went to the Café

Royal for a drink. Where I sat I was directly facing the clock set in the wall above the buffet, a round, plain clock with a face like that of an old-fashioned watch very much enlarged. My mind returned to the waitress; I remembered an evening in Prague when my wrist-watch had been stolen from me in a tramcar without my noticing it. My thoughts wandered on, and I found myself thinking that I was too old now for a wrist-watch; for some reason this seemed a perfectly sensible notion. But in that case—I was still paying very little attention to my thoughts—what sort of watch should I wear, for it was inconvenient to be without a watch? Then I saw dangling in the air a big, heavy watch such as the ploughmen used to wear when I was a boy. This troubled me, for what pocket could I keep it in? The watch settled the matter by dropping into my breast pocket, where it attached itself by a black, twisted cord to the top buttonhole of my coat, under the lapel. But this is a very juvenile arrangement, I told myself, wakening into another layer of daydream, though not into complete awakeness. Then, as if all these windings had been deliberately leading up to it, all at once I saw a boy's blue sailor suit with a yellow twisted hempen cord loosely knotted round the collar, and at the end of it a canary-yellow wooden whistle. The sailor suit startled me so much that I did not know what to do with it. Next moment I realised that I had worn it once; I could remember distinctly the feel and the smell of the smooth wooden whistle; it had a faint, fragrant smell. But I could not say when I had worn that suit, and the fact that after being buried for all these years it should come back now by such a tortuous and yet purposive road struck me as very strange. Yet it seemed still stranger that it could have disappeared at all, for the yellow whistle must have been one of the things which I loved most as a child, since even in memory I could feel the delight it had given me. Could some disaster have befallen the yellow whistle, so that I put it so completely out of my mind that it had never returned since? If that could happen once it might have happened hundreds of times.

I can still see the scarlet dress and the sailor suit; I can see the rough grey stones spotted with lichen on the top of the Castle, and a bedraggled gooseberry bush in a corner of the garden whose branches I lovingly fingered for hours; but I cannot bring back the feelings which I had for them, the sense of being magically close to them, as if they were magnets drawing me with a palpable power. Reasonable explanations can be found for these feelings; the fact that every object is new to a child, that he sees it without understanding it, or understands it with a different understanding from that of experience—different, for there may be fear in it, but there cannot be calculation or worry; or even the fact that he is closer to things, since his eyes are only two or three feet from the ground, not five or six. Grass, stones, and insects are twice as near to him as they will be after he has grown up, and when I try to re-create my early childhood it seems to me that it was focused on such things as these, and that I lived my life in a small, separate under-world, while the grown-ups walked on their long legs several feet above my head on a stage where every relation was different. I was dizzily lifted into that world, as into another dimension, when my father took me on his shoulders, so that I could see the roof of the byre from above or touch the lintel of the house door with my hand. But for most of the time I lived with whatever I found on the surface of the earth: the different kinds of grass, the daisies, buttercups, dandelions, bog cotton (we did not have many flowers), the stones and bits of glass and china, and the scurrying insects which made my stomach heave as I stared at them, unable to take my eyes away. These insects were all characters to me, interesting but squalid, with thoughts that could never be penetrated, inconceivable aims, perverse activities. I knew their names, which so exactly fitted them as characters: the Jenny Hunderlegs, the gavelock, the forkytail, the slater—the underworld of my little underworld, obsessing me, but forever beyond my reach. Some were not so horrible, such as the spider, impersonal compared with the others, whose progress was a terrifying dart or a grave, judge-like, swaying walk. Unlike the others, he was at home in the sun, and so did not need to scuttle; I thought of him as bearded and magistral. I could never bear to touch any of these creatures, though I watched them so closely that I seemed to be taking part in their life, which was like little fragments of night darting about in the sun; they often came into my dreams later, wakening me in terror. How many hours I must have spent staring with fixed loathing at these creatures! Yet I did not want to know anything about them; I merely wanted them away. Their presence troubled me as the mind is troubled in adolescence by the realisation of physical lust. The gavelocks and forkytails were my first intimation of evil, and associations of evil still cling round them for me, as, I fancy, for most people: popular imagery shows it. We cannot tell how much our minds are influenced for life by the fact that we see the world first at a range of two or three feet.

The insects, of course, were only a small part of that three-foot world; I think I must have passed through a phase of possession by them, com-paratively short. The grass was a reliable pleasure; the flowers were less dependable, and after I picked a dandelion one day and found it writhing with little angry, many-legged insects, the faces of the flowers took on a faithless look, until my mother taught me which could be relied upon. The crevices in stone walls were filled with secrets; a slab of hard cement on the wall on the house had a special meaning. Mud after new rain was delicious, and I was charmed by everything that flew, from the humble bee to the Willy Longlegs. At that stage the novelty of seeing a creature flying outweighed everything else. . . .

The distance of my eyes from the ground influenced my image of my father and mother too. I have a vivid impression of my father's cream-coloured moleskin breeches, which resisted elastically when I flung myself against them, and of my mother's skirt, which yielded, softly enveloping me. But I cannot bring back my mental impression of them, for it is overlaid by later memories in which I saw them as a man and a woman, like, or almost like, other men and women. I am certain that I did not see them like this at first; I never thought that they were like other men and women; to me they were fixed allegorical figures in a timeless landscape. Their allegorical changelessness made them more, not less, solid, as if they were condensed into something more real than humanity; as if the image 'mother' meant more than 'woman' and the image 'father' more than 'man'. It was the same with my brothers and sisters, my cousin Sutherland, and my aunt Maggie. We begin life not by knowing men and women, but a father and a mother, brothers and sisters. Men and women, and mankind in general, are secondary images, for we know them first as strangers; but our father and mother were never strangers to us, nor our brothers and sisters if we were the last born, as I was. When I was a child I must have felt that they had always been there, and I with them, since I could not account for myself; and now I can see them only as a stationary pattern, changing, yet always the same, not as a number of separate people all following the laws of their different natures. Where all was stationary my mother came first; she certainly had always been with me in a region which could never be known again. My father came next, more recognisably in my own time, yet rising out of changelessness like a rock out of the sea. My brothers and sisters were new creatures like myself, not in time (for time still sat on the wrist of each day with its wings folded), but in a vast, boundless calm. I could not have put all this into words then, but this is what I felt and what we all feel before we become conscious that time moves and that all things change. That world was a perfectly solid world, for the days did not undermine it but merely rounded it, or rather repeated it, as if there were only one day endlessly rising and setting. Our first childhood is the only time in our lives when we exist within immortality, and perhaps all our ideas of immortality are influenced by it. I do not mean that the belief in immortality is a mere rationalisation of childish impressions; I have quite other reasons for holding it. But we think and feel and believe immortally in our first few years, simply because time does not exist for us. We pay no attention to time until he tugs us by the sleeve or claps his policeman's hand on our shoulder; it is in our nature to ignore him, but he will not be ignored.

I can see my father quite clearly still with my later sight, though he has been dead for fifty years. He was a little, slight man with the soft brown beard of one who had never used a razor. His head was inclined sideways like the heads of statues of medieval saints; this had a natural cause, a contracted neck muscle; yet it seemed merely the outward mark of his character, which was gentle and meditative. His face was narrowish, with a long, delicate nose and large, fastidious lips almost hidden by his beard. He was slightly deaf and very embarrassed by it, and this may have been the reason why he was so fond of talking to himself. He would hold long conversations in the fields when no one was near; dialogues or monologues, I do not know which; but one could tell by the posture of his body and an occasional pensive wave of the hand that he was occupied. He was a religious man, but not strict or ostentatiously pious; he attended church irregularly but reverently; he often omitted grace before meals for long stretches; then he would remember and begin again. Every Sunday night he gathered us together to read a chapter of the Bible and kneel down in prayer. These Sunday nights are among my happiest memories; there was a feeling of complete security and union among us as we sat reading about David or Elijah. My father's prayer, delivered in a sort of mild chant while we knelt on the floor, generally ran on the same lines; at one point there always came the words, for which I waited, "an house not made with hands, eternal in the heavens". As a young man he had been saved, but he was not confident of his salvation, and I once heard him saying to my mother that he wished he was as certain of going to heaven as Jock M., a strict elder. I think there was a touch of irony in his words.

Edwin Muir, *An Autobiography*. The Hogarth Press, 1954.

JOHN FIRTH (1838–1922), was born in the township of Redland, part of the parish of Firth. His life was passed in the village of Finstown where he carried on business as joiner and cartwright. A student of botany, archaeology, and folk-lore, he published, when he was eighty years of age, an account of Orkney life, customs and character in the first half of the nineteenth century. This book, *Reminiscences of an Orkney Parish*, from which the following extract comes, is one of our island classics.

THE DWELLING HOUSE

IN the district of Redland the house of the cottar and that of the land-lord were very much alike, and, with few exceptions, consisted of only two rooms, a *but* and a *ben*, both doing duty as sleeping apartments, dining halls, and reception rooms, as well as providing accommodation for the household pets—a miscellaneous order, including dogs, pigs, geese, etc.

The outward aspect of these houses or huts, as they might more correctly be called, was dull and uninviting. The low-pitched, thatched roof was supported by walls three feet thick and not above six feet high, devoid of cement or lime and unbroken by windows. In more primitive times the stones for building purposes were gathered off the land, and were of a small size, but here and there in the walls a large boulder acted as a binder.

Though the Orcadian of those days did not go in for horticulture, nevertheless his dwelling was adorned with vegetation of the lower orders, lichens of varied hue hiding the unevenness of the masonry, and weeds flourishing abundantly in the thatch, while the chance ears of unthrashed bere or black oats readily sent up hardy sprouts, which waved green above his roof-tree. One of the houses in this district was built so near to a brae that the roof was easily accessible to the four-footed animals. On one occasion a neighbour's ox, being tempted by the plenteous tufts of growing corn, ventured on the roof to secure a bite, with the result that he plunged right through the thatch, and the cupples being wide apart, there was nothing to stay his fall, which resulted in a broken back and ultimate death.

The byre was usually built at the but-end of the house, and the one house door was often used as a byre door as well, but whether the cows entered by a separate door or not, in every case a door led from the dwelling house directly into the byre, and where the other farm build-ings were connected to the byre the farmer could walk from his ben-end in a direct line through byre, stable, and barn.

The entrance door was made of deal boards nailed to the back bars with wooden pegs, the orderly arrangement of which was the only attempt at ornamentation or finish. These pegs or pins, as they were commonly called, were made with a square head, which was set diamond-wise in the outside of the door. On the inside the ends of the pins were wedged or orrowed to render them secure. Locks and elaborate door handles were unknown, a wooden latch with string of tanned hide or alum skin being the only fastening; while for extra security a wooden running bar notched on one edge took the place of the modern lock, the key being simply a rod with a crook on one end, which reached the bar through a small hole in the door. The hinges, too, were of wood, and were home-made. They were nailed to the jambs with large nails made by the local blacksmith, as were all the nails then in common use. Though knockers were unheard of, and indeed the ceremony of knocking dispensed with altogether, each having free access to his neighbour's house, the visitor was loudly announced by the unmusical creak of the wooden hinges, which could easily be heard half-a-mile away; and should the creaking be prevented by a liberal application of grease, the household pets never failed to set up a chorus of welcome. In every case the house door was placed in the but-end of the house near to the gable, and opened into that part designated 'oot-by', which in addition to being the entrance hall, served as a convenient place for rearing calves. These were usually tied to the gable end just beyond the byre door. In the further corner the brood sow and her litter of grizes were separated from the calves by a rough flagstone set on edge to form a pen, while along the side wall two flagstones were set up to form a 'paetie-neuk', where the day's supply of yarpha and good 'coal-peats' was stored. Aloft along the gable ran two horizontal bars of wood, eighteen inches apart, laced or 'wupped' with straw simmons. This was the *hallan* or hens' roost, where—

> "Chanticleer shook aff the poodry snaw,
> And hailed the morning wi' a cheer—
> A cottage rousing craw."

The only division between all these animals and the but-end or kitchen was the 'back'—a low, crow-stepped wall about eighteen inches thick, and not more than four or five feet high at the highest point. Down at the floor a hole about one foot square passed through the 'back', and in front of this hole was placed the back-peat—a wet, sandy peat, against which the fire of coal peats was built, supported on either side with heavy yarpha peats. When the fire was built up in the morning a fresh back peat was set up, the ashes were pushed through this hole to the oot-by end, and were confined within a circle of wet sandy peats, which were broken up or hacked with an eetch. The hot ashes soon reduced the sandy peats to a fine powder, and this mixture was cleared off every morning, and carried in caisies to the byres for bedding to the cows, instead of straw, which in those days was a scarce commodity. The frequent scooping up of the ashes soon made a hollow in the earthen floor. This was termed the assie-pow. Housewives had an art of their own for preserving live 'coals' to light the morning fire, matches and paraffin being then unknown. Half-burnt peats were laid flat on the hearth stone and covered with cold ashes. If by any mischance the raking peats burned out and a 'gleed', or a half-burnt peat, had to be borrowed from a neighbour, it was considered unlucky if the borrower caught her neighbour in the act of churning, for no butter would be got. The burnt peat was always given, but should it fail to light the fire and she return again, the evil influence of her visit was counteracted by her taking a turn at the churn.

Cooking was of the simplest kind. The only utensils in use were the brand-iron for bannock baking, the yetlin' (girdle) of cast-iron for baking sowan scones, and the three-toed pots of different sizes, varying from the muckle pot of ten gallons to the peerie pot for the bairns' milk gruel. These cooking utensils were suspended over the fire by a long iron chain or by four folds of straw simmons wound together, with five or six iron links next to the fire. Any danger of fire in the simmons was prevented by the coating of wet soot which streamed down from the roof. The pots were hung from this suspender by a crook, which was linked up or down according to the degree of heat required for cooking. The chain or simmons was fixed to a round stick of Highland birk, which crossed the house just above the fire, either end being built into the side wall just at the eaves or easings. This stick was called the pauntree, and may yet be seen in some of the older farmhouses, which have been renovated and fitted with more modern fireplaces. The *lum*, made of boards, and projecting eighteen inches above the ridge, was nailed to the cupples in the centre of the roof, and formed an aperture two feet square. This was the only outlet for the smoke, while it served the purpose of a window as well as being the only means of ventilation. The clouds of smoke eddied and whirled some time through the air of the room before they reached the lum, it being placed near the oot-by gable, and not over the fire, as one would naturally expect. Conflicting draughts from the doors sent the strong-smelling peat smoke through every corner of the dwelling, and it may be that it acted as a disinfectant as well as a deodoriser, where man and beast were herded together in such limited space.

WALTER TRAILL DENNISON (1826–94) was a farmer throughout his life in his native island of Sanday. He became keenly interested in the oral traditions and the ancient language of the old people, likely soon to be forgotten, and with the object of preserving the Orkney dialect he wrote a series of tales in prose and verse. These were published in 1880, under the title, *The Orcadian Sketch-Book*. Dennison's spelling causes some difficulty, but the stories are lively and full of interest. They form a unique contribution to our island literature, and one is reprinted here.

THE SELKIE THAT DEUD NO' FORGET

AE time langsine, Mansie Meur wus pickan' lempeds i' the ebb, on the wast side o' Hacksness i' Sanday, whin he wus stunned tae hear some wey amang the rocks a unco' ceurious soond. Sometimes hid wus like a bothy i' terrable pain, makin' meen; an' dan hid wad mak' a lood soond like the root o' a deean' coo. An' dan again de soond wad dee awa' tae a laich an' maist peetifu' meen, as gin hid been a bothy oot-mucht i' a bought o' the wark. The soond wus sae awfu' peetifu', hid meed Mansie think lang tae hear hid. Mansie could see naethin' for a peerie while bit a muckle selkie closs in at the rocks, rakin' his heed abeun de skreuf o' the water, an' leukan' wi' baith his een i'tae a geo a peerie bit awa'. An' Mansie noticed that the selkie wus no' faer'd, niver dookid, an' niver teuk his e'e aff o' that geo. Mansie geed ower a muckle rock 'at lay atween him an' that geo; an' there, i' a cunyo o' the geo, he saw a mither selkie lyan' i' a' the trouble o' her callowin'-pains. An' hid wus her that meed a' the sair meen an' lood yowlin'; an' the faither selkie lay i' the sea watchin' his marrow i' her trouble. Mansie steud an' watched her teu, an' said it wus peetifu' tae see what the peur dumb animal suffered. An' there he steud, a bit aff, till sheu callowed twa bonnie selkie calves, that wur nee seuner on the rock or dey grippid for de pap. Mansie t'ought tae himsel' the calf hides wad mak' a bonnie waistco't tae him; an' he ran tae whar dey wur a' t'ree lyan'. The peur mither selkie rowed hersel' ower the face o' de rock i'tae the sea; bit her twa birds hed no' wit tae flee. Sae Mansie grippid dem baith. An' dan hid wus sae winderfu' tae see the atfares o' the mither selkie. She teuk sic' t'ought for her young. Sheu rowed aboot an' aboot i' the sea, an' baeted hersel' wi' her megs, like a t'ing distracted. An' dan sheu wad climmer ap wi' her fore megs on de face o' de rock, an' glower'd i' Mansie's face, wi' a luck sae terrably peetifu', hid wad hae melted a he'rt o' steen tae seen her. The faither selkie wus ga'n the sam' wey, only he wad no' come sae near Mansie. Mansie turned tae gang awa' wi' the twa selkie birds i' his erms,—dey wur sookin' at his co't as gin dey been at the mither's breest,—whin he heard the selkie mither gae a groan sae dismal an' how, an' sae human like, that hid geed stra'cht tae his he'rt, an' fairly owercam' him. He luckid aboot, an' saw the mither selkie lyan' on her side, wi' her heed on the rock; an' he saw—as seur as iver he saw a t'ing on earth—the tares feeman' fae baith her e'en. Tae see nater wirkan' sae sair i' the peur dumb crater, he could nae bide hid mair. Sae he looted doon an' passed baith the peerie selkies on the rock. The mither teuk dem i' her megs, an' clespid dem tae her bosom, as gin sheu been a bothy wi' a 'bairn. An' sheu luckid i' Mansie's face;—O! sic' a blithe luck the selkie gae him. Sheu deud Mansie geud tae see her. For dat day the selkie deud ivery t'ing but spaek.

Mansie wus dan a young man; an' a while efter dat he married. An' a lang while efter he married, whin his bairns wur groun-ap folk, he geed tae bide on the wast side o' Eday. Ae bonnie e'enin', Mansie geed tae fish sillo's aff o' a oot-lyan' rock. He wus a ootflow rock, that ye could only gang tae dry-shod wi' low water. The fish wad no' tak' ava' for a peerie while; bit whin he begood tae flou, sheu set on an' teuk brawly, sae that Mansie steud an' hauled whill he filled his sea-cubbie. The fish teuk sae bonnie, that i' his feurceness tae fish he forgot the gate he hed tae gang. An' whin he cam' tae gang heem, he wus sairly stunned tae see the trink atween him an' the land fairly flou'd ower, an' the sea sae deep he wad taen him abeun de heed. Mansie cried an' better cried; bit he wus far fae ony hoose, an' nee bothy heard his cries. The water raise an' raise, cam' ap abeun his knees, abeun his henches, ap tae his oxters; an' miny a sair sich gae he, as de water cam' aye hicher an' nearer tae his chin. He cried whill he wus trapple-hers', an' he could cry nee mair. An' dan he gae ap a' hup' o' life, an' saw naething afore him bit dismal daeth. An' dan, as de sea wus comin' roond his hass, an' comin' noos an' dans i' peerie lippers tae his mooth, jeust as he f'and the sea beginnan' tae lift him fae the rock,—summin' grippid him bae the neck o' the co't an' whippid him aff o' his feet. He kent no' what hid wus, or whar he wus, till he f'and his feet at the boddam, whar he could wad ashore i' safety. An' whin de craeter 'at hed haud o' him passed him, he wadded tae the dry land. He luckid whar he cam' fae, an' saw a muckle selkie swimman' tae the rock, whar sheu dookid, teuk ap his cubbie o' fish, an' swam wi'd tae the land. He wadded oot an' teuk the cubbie fu' o' fish oot o' her mooth; an' he said wi' a' his he'rt, 'Geud bliss the selkie that deus no' forget'. An' sheu luckid tae him, as gin, if sheu could hae spoken, sheu wad hae said,

'Ae geud turn meets anither'. Sheu wus the sam' selkie that he saw callowan' on Hacksness, forty years afore. He said he wad hae kent her mitherly luck amang a thoosan'. Bit sheu wus groun a arkmae. Sae that wus the selkie that deud no' forget. I wiss' a' bothy may mind on what's geud, as weel as that selkie.

GLOSSARY

a'bothy: everybody
arkmae: a very large old seal
'at: that
atfares: behaviour
bought: a fit
callowed: calved
cubbie: small basket
cunyo: a corner, a crevice
dan: then
de: the
deu: do
deud: did
feurce: fierce, rash
geo: a cave, a creek
hass: the neck
how: hollow

laich: low
lippers: ripples
looted: bent the body down
luck: to look
meen: moan
megs: the paws, or semi-fins, of the seal
ootmoucht: quite tired out, exhausted
oxters: armpits
root: to roar loudly
selkie: seal
sheu: she
skreuf: the surface, the outside crust
trapple-hers': hoarse in the throat
trink: a channel
whill: till, until, sometimes while
wus: was

JOHN SPENCE was a native of the parish of Birsay, Orkney, where he farmed the lands of Overabist. He received a limited education in a little Hillside school, but his native intelligence, memory, and powers of observation enabled him to become an authority on the flora of his parish, on local history and genealogy, and on the old Orkney dialect, the Norn. He died in 1933 at the age of seventy-six.

LIFE AND WORK IN MOORLAND ORCADIA IN DAYS OF OLD

The Weather

IN the good old days before meteorology and weather-glasses were in vogue, and when, nevertheless, there was often better weather than now, Moorland Orcadia, the eastern section of the parish of Birsay, had a meteorology all its own. When the sea cried at the Costa shore it was sure to presage snow; but when the roaring was shifted the least bit eastward to the Röst o' Burgar it was equally sure to presage or foretell sunshine. The year 1902 or 1903, I am not sure which, had the songs of the North Sea to great excess; and there was somewhat of winter every month of the year. July and August, the most likely months for warmth, had, the one a hail shower, the other a hoar-frost.

The School

The academy to which I was sent was a 'lang Scots mile' away across the heather, and I began to go at four years of age. We had to carry a peat for the school fire, too. The teacher in that academy on the moor taught arithmetic, grammar, composition, mathematics, navigation, Euclid, Latin, and mechanics; algebra too, and in all of those they who could waded in. I remember Dr Kerr, I think his name was, examining us one day. He was clad in a white duck jacket. In summer in those days duck jackets were common boys' wear. In winter they sometimes sported 'tweestie', that is, homespun cloth of white and black native wool with the threads interwoven.

This 'kelter', as it was called, was the common wear in earlier days, but it was getting out of date first I remember. The head-dress worn with this russet 'strood' was what was then called the 'Scotch bannet'. The holiday coat of south-country cloth was called the 'wide coat'. This garment was fastened about the person with large metal buttons.

But about life in the schooldays of old, of which we were just speaking, the peat referred to was often put to other purposes than mere firing. When a boy or girl offended, the punishment they sometimes got was to hold a peat straight up in the hand, and woe betide the refractory student who let it decline in any measure from the perpendicular. A smart rap on the weary elbow soon brought the whole plumb up. Yet, in spite of those, and many more such-like facts of my student days, I will say this for the two teachers in that moorland academy, that they were first-class teachers both. The faults of discipline or 'niction', to give the right word, were faults—if they were faults—of the time. I learned a good many things in this school that I might not have learned anywhere else, and the teachers were men in many ways ahead of their time.

The Hill Dykes

When the seed-time was over in late spring every available man was told off to 'bigg ap the slaps i' the hill-dyke'. For all the young kye, and for that matter the horses, and even swine, were put to the hills for the summer. And many a 'slap' other than the regular entries were made by those ancient 'nowte bestial'. So that for a fortnight or so in the first of each summer the earth-dykes round each 'toonship' had to be put 'i' right fettle'. Like the broad walls of Babylon, those old hill-dykes are sadly broken down now. In a few places they may be seen standing well up still, as above the Loan on the north-east end of Greeny Hill. The eastern side of this hill has been cut over for peats, but shows no cart-tracks, the peats having been carried off in 'forsals', or 'maisies', on horses' backs. As showing the warm summer prevalent in the olden time, I have heard that the tenant of Tufta in Twatt toonship was half-way up the 'Teeve', the western slope of Greeny Hill, with his horses going to 'lead' home peats one fine sunny summer morn before he put on his 'sark'!

The Lammas Market

The great holiday of the year in Moorland Orcadia, as indeed in all Orkney, was the Kirkwall Lammas Market. I remember my father telling of his being at this great world-fair. As he wanted, like most young fellows of the olden time, to see it to the full, he decided to stay in the capital overnight. So he tried for decent lodgings for the night and at last got a bed in lodgings kept by a good old man who was familiarly called Tammy Omand. If I remember rightly, he said there were fourteen of them in one 'beul', with a double blanket stretched over them where they lay side by side! Those ancient 'Lammas Beuls', of which so much has been said, adversely and otherwise, were a necessity of the olden days, with no roads or swift traffic to and fro, save on horseback.

But it was not for holiday alone that Orcadia's Lammas Fair was held.

It was the great horse market of Orkney. The horses had to have their beul also, if not sold. So there was a place called 'the park' in which they were put overnight. My grandfather had a horse put in the park. Sometime during the night his horse had been relieved of a beautiful spotted hair halter, for which a very ordinary one had been substituted. Poor greedy specimens of humanity even yet covet halters and other things in various surreptitious ways.

Speaking of hair halters, in the olden time a good horse was expected to keep himself in tether with the hair of his tail and mane. This hair rope, which I have seen used in early days, was spun on a home-made machine called a 'winchou'. The ropes thus made were beautiful, but they could not be used safely with an iron stake on account of the recoil. Sometimes horses were killed in that way. Another more elaborate machine for making hair rope was what was called a 'tammar-spindle'. This was a more ancient device, which I have heard spoken of but have never seen. Nor can I now recall how it was made, or how it wrought.

Peat-cutting

Peat-cutting was carried on here in the olden time in much the same manner, and with much the same implements or tools, as at the present day. The 'ritting knife', the 'moor spade', and the 'tusker' are perhaps the same as in the days of Torf Einar, who was credited with teaching the Orcadian of the Viking days how to utilise peat fuel. But I rather think that the native Picts of Orkney must have used peat fuel before the Norse came among them.

The work of securing peat fuel is much the same as it always was. First rit and dell the bank, then with 'tusker' in hand at the top of the peat-bank cut the peats for a partner at the bottom 'takin' oot'. The first of May was considered as the ideal time to begin cutting peats. When cut and set on the bank face, they stood for a week or more. Then they were 'casten oot'. Then when they were sufficiently dry on the upper side, they were raised three in each 'raising'. Some time after, when nearly dry, they were put together in 'bullans', or 'hobbles'. Not until all these processes had been gone through were they fit to carry home to stack. In the olden time, as we have already said, the peats were carried home in 'leads' on horseback.

The peat-cutting day first I mind was a great day. Early in the morning the work was started. After two or three hours a halt was called. The whole crew sat down on the heather and had breakfast from a pail of hot 'milk-gruel'. This was invariably the dish for breakfast. Then cutting again till dinner-time. Those near the moss went home for dinner. This was more varied. Broth about 'reestid mutton', with perhaps a bowl of brose made of oatmeal and the fat that had risen atop of the broth in the pot was first in evidence. And some of the flesh also; though this was more kept for the supper. After dinner there was the final bout at peat-cutting; the last peat being a square block of moss three or four times the size of the ordinary peat. This was called the 'supper-peat'. It was taken out and set carefully on end on the top of the bank.

The fire on the hearth by which I write has not gone out for ages. The fire here now is not 'strange fire', for every night since I remember the 'raking peats' have been covered with coals and hot 'ase' to kindle the fire in the morning. Indeed, in the old time it would have been held a calamity to have the fire gone out. I have heard an old man speak of the advantage of having put on a fire in a vacant house, thereby getting a claim in right. The home-fires had always to be kept perpetually alive.

Harvest

In the early years, when harvest came in September, the 'hairst-time' was the most joyous time in Moorland Orcadia. When the hills put on their robes of imperial purple, and the corn was slowly ripening in the quiet sunlight, there was an inexpressible charm in the scene, the speaking silence of the miracle of morn, most seen and felt and heard in the harvest-time. During the last half-century, the Orkney weather on the whole has roughened immensely. Warm springs, when walking barefoot was the order of the day for the whole summer through, were common then. Should there come a colder snap for a few days, 'sprettows' or 'ceutows' would be put on. The first of these were stockings without the soles; the second sock-lengths reaching just above the 'ceuts', also without soles. They were fastened by a loop on the toe next the big toe. I do not think I have seen a man or woman, native or 'ferrylouper', sporting either 'sprettows' or 'ceutows' for fifty years!

I have seen the reaping hook, the scythe, the manual reaper, and the binder used in harvesting, and have to some extent wrought them all.

But the joy of harvest has gone these two or three years past. Gone with the good old Orkney weather I remember. 'Breaking' of corn sheaves, each one by itself, 'dissing' of oat sheaves in twenty-fives, 'drilty i' the yaird slap', 'the strae dog', 'the muckle-supper', 'the mullyou corn', and all the rest—all have vanished—'and these are ancient things'.

John Spence, *Proceedings of the Orkney Antiquarian Society.*
Vol. II (Session 1923–24).

Some Orcadian Poets

EDWIN MUIR is probably best known for his verse, and these examples are taken from his *Collected Poems*, published by Faber and Faber in 1960.

CHILDHOOD

Long time he lay upon the sunny hill,
  To his father's house below securely bound.
Far off the silent, changing sound was still,
  With the black islands lying thick around.

He saw each separate height, each vaguer hue,
  Where the massed islands rolled in mist away,
And though all ran together in his view
  He knew that unseen straits between them lay.

Often he wondered what new shores were there.
  In thought he saw the still light on the sand,
The shallow water clear in tranquil air,
  And walked through it in joy from strand to strand.

Over the sound a ship so slow would pass
  That in the black hill's gloom it seemed to lie.
The evening sound was smooth like sunken glass,
  And time seemed finished ere the ship passed by.

Grey tiny rocks slept round him where he lay,
  Moveless as they, more still as evening came,
The grasses threw straight shadows far away,
  And from the house his mother called his name.

HORSES

Those lumbering horses in the steady plough,
On the bare field—I wonder why, just now,
They seemed terrible, so wild and strange,
Like magic power on the stony grange.

Perhaps some childish hour has come again,
When I watched fearful, through the blackening rain,
Their hooves like pistons in an ancient mill
Move up and down, yet seem as standing still.

Their conquering hooves which trod the stubble down
Were ritual that turned the field to brown,
And their great hulks were seraphim of gold,
Or mute ecstatic monsters on the mould.

And oh the rapture, when, one furrow done,
They marched broad-breasted to the sinking sun!
The light flowed off their bossy sides in flakes;
The furrows rolled behind like struggling snakes.

But when at dusk with steaming nostrils home
They came, they seemed gigantic in the gloam,
And warm and glowing with mysterious fire
That lit their smouldering bodies in the mire.

Their eyes as brilliant and as wide as night
Gleamed with a cruel apocalyptic light.
Their manes the leaping ire of the wind
Lifted with rage invisible and blind.

Ah, now it fades! it fades! and I must pine
Again for that dread country crystalline,
Where the blank field and the still-standing tree
Were bright and fearful presences to me.

ONE FOOT IN EDEN

One foot in Eden still, I stand
And look across the other land.
The world's great day is growing late,
Yet strange these fields that we have planted
So long with crops of love and hate.
Time's handiworks by time are haunted,
And nothing now can separate
The corn and tares compactly grown.
The armorial weed in stillness bound
About the stalk; these are our own.
Evil and good stand thick around
In the fields of charity and sin
Where we shall lead our harvest in.

Yet still from Eden springs the root
As clean as on the starting day.
Time takes the foliage and the fruit
And burns the archetypal leaf
To shapes of terror and of grief
Scattered along the winter way.
But famished field and blackened tree
Bear flowers in Eden never known.
Blossoms of grief and charity
Bloom in these darkened fields alone.
What had Eden ever to say
Of hope and faith and pity and love
Until was buried all its day
And memory found its treasure trove?
Strange blessings never in Paradise
Fall from these beclouded skies.

THE LATE SWALLOW

Leave, leave your well-loved nest,
Late swallow, and fly away.
Here is no rest
For hollowing heart and wearying wing.
Your comrades all have flown
To seek their southern paradise
Across the great earth's downward sloping side,
And you are alone.
Why should you cling
Still to the swiftly ageing narrowing day?
Prepare;
Shake out your pinions long untried
That now must bear you there where you would be
Through all the heavens of ice;
Till falling down the homing air
You light and perch upon the radiant tree.

ROBERT RENDALL (born 1898), has spent almost all his life as a business-man in Kirkwall, but much of his spare time has been given to marine research and to literary work. His study of the Orkney beaches led him to compile an exhaustive catalogue of the marine mollusca of Orkney, which was published in 1956 in the Proceedings of the Royal Society of Edinburgh. A later work is a series of essays, entitled *Orkney Shore* (1960).

In his native county he is best known for his volumes of poetry, *Country Sonnets* (1946), *Orkney Variants* (1951), and *Shore Poems* (1957).

LOST SELF

To be what I have been but am no more
Or find the shadow of what once was plain
I pace the margin of this haunted shore
Where rocks and stones and echoing cliffs retain
Lost ecstasies, and shouts of natural joy.
Back through a maze of transient gains and griefs
I pick my steps to seek a phantom boy
Who flits from ledge to ledge on these black reefs.
But all the pools have unfamiliar grown
Since those forgotten years, nor can I trace
The distant footprints there that are my own,
Which time can never touch nor tides efface.
  Of this strange world the meaning who can tell,
  Receding thus from those that know it well?

SALT I' THE BLUID

A'm bydan heem, 'at geed for lang
  Ruggan afore the mast,
Yet times me thowts they taak a spang
  Aff tae the wild Nor'wast.

On winter nights I whiles can feel
  Me cottage gaan adrift,
An' wance again I grip the wheel
  Tae the sea-swaal's aisy lift.

Whan lood swaps gouster[1] at the door,
　An' the nort' wind tirls the sneck,
Full canvas on, we drive afore,
　As whaalbacks[2] sweep the deck.

Spier no for siklike ferlies proof!
　Things chance when nights are lang:
The very timmers o' the roof
　Creak as we dunt alang.

CRAGSMAN'S WIDOW

'He was aye vaigan b' the shore,
　An' climman doun the craigs,
Swappan amang the auks,
　Or taakan whitemaa aiggs.

'It's six year bye come Lammas,
　Sin' he gaed afore the face,
An' nane but an aald dune wife
　Was left tae work the place.

'Yet the sun shines doun on a' thing,
　The links are bonnie and green,
An' the sea keeps ebban an' flowan
　As though it had never been.'

[1] gouster: storm violently.
[2] whaalbacks: long smooth waves (lit. whale-backs).

GEORGE MACKAY BROWN (born 1921), a native of Stromness, was educated there and at Newbattle Abbey College and Edinburgh University. While at Newbattle he came under the influence of Edwin Muir, who said of him, 'He has the gift of imagination and the gift of words: the poet's endowment'. A volume of verse, *The Storm and other poems*, was published in 1954 and won favourable recognition. This has been followed by another two volumes of poems, also of fine quality—*Loaves and Fishes* (1959), and *The Year of the Whale* (1965).

THE STORM

What blinding storm there was! How it
Flashed with a leap and lance of nails,
    Lurching, O suddenly
    Over the lambing hills,

Hounding me there! With sobbing lungs
I reeled past kirk and ale-house
    And the thousand candles
    Of gorse round my mother's yard,

And down the sand shot out my skiff
Into the long green jaws, while deep
    In summer's sultry throat
    Dry thunder stammered.

Swiftly the sail drew me over
The snarling Sound, scudding before
    The heraldic clouds now
    Rampant all around.

The sea—organ and harps—wailed miserere;
Swung me in fluent valleys, poised
    On icy yielding peaks
    Hissing spume, until

Rousay before me, the stout mast
Snapped, billowing down helpless sail.
    What evil joy the storm
    Seized us! plunged and spun!

And flung us, skiff and man (wave-crossed, God-lost)
On a rasp of rock! . . . The shore breakers,
    Stained chancel lights,
    Cluster of mellow bells,

Crossed hands, scent of holy water. . . .
The storm danced over all that night,
    Loud with demons, but I
    Safe in Brother Colm's cell.

Next morning in tranced sunshine
The corn lay squashed on every hill;
    Tang and tern were strewn
    Among highest pastures.

I tell you this, my son: after
That Godsent storm, I find peace here
    These many years with
    The Gray Monks of Eynhallow.

THE FIVE VOYAGES OF ARNOR

I, Arnor the red poet, made
Four voyages out of Orkney.

The first was to Ireland.
That was a viking cruise.
Thorlief came home with one leg.
We left Guthorm in Ulster,
His blood growing cold by the saint's well.
Rounding Cape Wrath, I made my first poem.

Norway hung fogs about me.
I won the girl Ragnhild
From Paul her brother, after
I beat him at draughts, three games to two.
Out of Bergen, the waves made her sick.
She was uglier than I expected, still
I made five poems about her
That men sing round the bench at Yule.
She filled my quiet house with words.

A white wave threw me on Iceland.
Sweyn's skull is there (my brother) in a round howe.
Rolf rode him down
In Thingvellir, after the council, and rode on
Through villages, red-hooved, to the sea
Far from Inga his sister
And the lawless cry in the cradle, Inga's and Sweyn's,
And the farm at Rangower . . .
They put an axe in my hand, the edge turned north,
Those women, the shapes in black.
Lilies and snow on the hill above Broadfirth
And Rangower silent . . .
In Unst two nights, coming home,
We drank the ale and discussed new metres.
For the women, I reddened the axe at a dog's throat.

I went the blue road to Jerusalem
With fifteen ships in a brawling company
Of poets, warriors, and holy men.
A hundred swords were broken that voyage.
Prayer on a hundred white wings
Rose every morning. The Mediterranean
Was richer by a hundred love songs.
We saw the hills where God walked
And the last hill, where his feet were broken.
At Rome, the earl left us. His hooves beat north.

Three Fridays sick of the black cough
Tomorrow I make my last voyage.
I should have suffered this thing
In Dublin, Micklegarth, Narbonne
(A bright sword in the storm of swords)
But here, at Hamnavoe, a pillow is under my head.
May all things be done in order.
The priest has given me oil and bread, a sweet cargo.
Ragnhild my daughter will cross my hands.
The boy Ljot must ring the bell.
I have said to Erling Saltfingers: *Drop my harp*
Through a green wave, off Yesnaby,
Next time you row to the lobsters.

APPENDIX

FACTS and FIGURES

The County of Orkney is a group of about sixty-five islands which extend fifty miles north-north-eastwards.

The population in 1961 was 18,650.

The area of the county is 376.3 square miles or 240,848 acres, compared with Shetland's 550.5 square miles or 352,337 acres.

Orkney is separated from Caithness by the Pentland Firth, 6½ miles wide at the narrowest.

North Ronaldsay is separated from Sumburgh Head, Shetland, by 50 miles of open sea.

The area of the Orkney Mainland, the largest island of the group, is about 202 square miles.

Hoy, the most 'Highland' looking of the Isles, is the second largest. Its area is about 57 square miles.

The highest elevation in the county is Ward Hill, Hoy which is 1,565 feet above sea-level.

The cliffs of Hoy attain a height of 1,140 feet and are the highest perpendicular sea cliffs in Great Britain.

The highest elevation on the Orkney Mainland is Ward Hill in Orphir—881 feet.

The highest hill in the North Isles is Blotchniefield, Rousay—821 feet.

The Old Man of Hoy stands 450 feet high—the height of St Paul's Cathedral.

Harray is Orkney's only parish without a seaboard.

The latitude of Kirkwall is approximately 59° North, and its longitude, 3° West.

At Kirkwall on 22 June, the sun rises at 3.10 a.m. and sets at 9.26 p.m. Greenwich Mean Time, thus being above the horizon for 18 hours 16 minutes.

The ruins of the Neolithic dwellings at Scara Brae were exposed after a violent storm in 1850. An Australian, Professor V. Gordon Childe, was mainly responsible for the excavation of Scara Brae between 1927 and 1930.

Orkney's earliest lighthouse was established at North Ronaldsay in 1789; Pentland Skerries came into service in 1794; and Sule Skerry, regarded as the most isolated lighthouse in Britain, in 1895.

Scapa Flow was mapped as a proposed roadstead for Line-of-Battle ships in 1812. In 1905 it was earmarked as a safe anchorage for the Fleet. It became an operational base in the First World War. The base at Lyness was closed in March, 1957.

The first issue of *The Orcadian*—four pages, price 2d.—came out in November, 1854. It contained news of the siege of Sebastopol in the Crimean War.

The first Orkney-owned car was brought to the islands in 1903.

The first Orkney motor-bus service, between Kirkwall and Stromness, was operated in 1905.

The busiest period of the herring fishing in Stronsay occurred just before the First World War. There were five curing stations on Papa Stronsay and a further fifteen at Whitehall village. At the peak period, 300 fishing boats, employing about 2,400 fishermen, were working out from Stronsay.

Lord Kitchener was drowned close to Marwick Head on 5 June, 1916 together with his staff and seven hundred officers and men of H.M.S. *Hampshire*.

The battleship H.M.S. *Vanguard* blew up while at anchor in Scapa Flow on 9 July, 1917, with the loss of almost all the officers and men of her company.

The Imperial German Navy was scuttled in Scapa Flow on 21 June, 1919. Seventy-four ships went down, including eleven battleships.

The Kitchener memorial on the 287-foot Marwick Head was unveiled in July, 1926.

The Churchill Causeway ('The Barriers') linking South Ronaldsay and Burray to the Orkney Mainland was formally opened on 12 May, 1945. Ten-ton and five-ton concrete blocks were used in its construction. The longest barrier is No. 2 and is 0.431 mile. The greatest depth of water the Barriers cross is 54 feet.

A memorial plaque, commemorating the loss of the battleship *Royal Oak* was unveiled in 1948 in the north aisle of St Magnus Cathedral.

The annual Stromness 'Shopping Week' (gala week) was inaugurated in 1949.

One hundred whales were stranded in the Bay of Holland, Stronsay, on 22 April, 1950.

The Great Gale of 15 January, 1952 caused £500,000 farming damage to Orkney, and the Great Gale of 31 January, 1953 wrecked Kirkwall's sea front.

Orkney's television station at Netherbutton came into service on 22 December, 1958.

INDEX

Bold figures are used to indicate a photograph or illustration